YOU NEED TO GET OUT MORE

Four Practices for Hospitable Living

Mark Feldmeir

ISBN-13: 978-1479228218 (print)
Also available as a Kindle eBook. For a list of additional stores and formats please visit www.markfeldmeir.com.

Published by Mark Feldmeir, Carlsbad, California 92009
Publishing Services by SellBox: www.sellbox.com
Original Photography by Louise Leclerc
Cover design by Sarah Nance
Gate sketch by Yolanda Zuniga

Contents

Acknowledgments

The author wishes to thank the following who have worked so generously to see this work into print—

David Wogahn at SellBox, whose friendship and wisdom fueled the vision, whose expertise in digital publishing carried this project from vision to completion, and whose own commitment to practicing the hospitable life has served as treasured inspiration.

Sarah Nance, who has generously shared her gift of graphic design to create a compelling cover that inspires us all to *get out more*.

Susan Herrmann and Rev. Martha Wingfield, who were among the first to read the original manuscript and whose wise counsel helped to inform the final draft.

Julie Reboulet, who painstakingly edited the manuscript while juggling the endless responsibilities and adventures of motherhood.

The people of San Dieguito United Methodist Church, whose commitment to the hospitable life is on display every day, in ways that continue to transform the neighborhood and light the world.

Introduction

WE ARE STANDING on the littered corner of Sixth and San Pedro in Downtown Los Angeles, otherwise known as "Ground Zero" of Skid Row, the capital tent city of America's homeless population, where more than 4,300 men, women and children make their home. We've just finished our work at the Central City Outreach Center, building a small classroom for an afterschool program for children living on Skid Row. We're making the half-mile walk to our car when a stranger on the corner steps abruptly into our path and demands, "Where you from?"

After eight hours of hammering nails and hanging drywall, it becomes immediately clear that this random encounter will prove to be the most important work of our day.

When I tell him that we've come from San Diego for the weekend to work at the Center, he sizes me up, reaches out his hand for mine and says, "We are real people, you know? People come through here every day, but they don't even see us." He points to two women who have just crossed the street ahead of us and says, "Those women can't even look at me. I ask them where they're from, and what do they do? They just look the other way and keep walking. They can't even look at me."

For the next ten minutes we get to know this very real person who calls himself "Supreme." He's in his late twenties, a native of New Orleans who washed up on the shores of Skid Row more than six years ago after the Storm. All that he owns is contained in the two large trash bags he holds in each hand. He tells us his story of once having – and suddenly losing – everything. He is the Prodigal, he says, who wandered far from home, squandering his father's blessing along the way. He used to sing in his father's gospel choir with his brother and sisters, which is why they call him Supreme. But he's now been on the streets so long that nobody knows where he is. "I have made my mistakes," he confesses. "It's my own damn fault I'm here. But I'm trying real hard to make it right."

Supreme has just showered for the first time in a week, a small luxury offered by the Union Rescue Mission to those who can pass a drug urine test. Three months into his sobriety, he dreams of going home. "I get three meals a day here," he says. "If I stay sober, they give me a bed at the mission. I'm getting what I need here," he says, "but the problem is—this ain't home."

Later that night I think about Supreme and recall that scene in the movie *Patch Adams*, where Hunter reflects on his life journey and his struggle to find love and acceptance in the world. He says,

> All of life is a coming home. Salesmen, secretaries, coal miners, beekeepers, sword swallowers, all of us. All the restless hearts of the world, all trying to find a way home. It's hard to describe... Picture yourself walking for days in the driving snow; you don't even know you're walking in circles. The heaviness of your legs in the drifts, your shouts disappearing into the wind. How small you can feel, and how far away home can be. Home. The dictionary defines it as both a place of origin and a... destination.

Where is home for you?

It's been said that "Home is where the heart is." That "Home is where you hang your hat." That "Home is where you can say anything you like because no one listens to you anyway." Robert Frost said, "Home is where, when you have to go there, they have to let you in."

But the kind of home that most of us are searching for is not merely a house, nor is it simply a particular place on a map. The kind of home you and I are apt to be searching for is that place where we find and share the unconditional welcome and boundless compassion of the people we happen to encounter there, wherever we happen to be. Some might describe that experience as having found "community," or a sense of belonging.

Because it's intimately tied to both people and place, I prefer to think of home as a neighborhood, where our lives flow freely, fearlessly into the lives of those around us, as wave flows into wave; and where we are anchored to the place, the land, the space we share, to the extent that we feel responsible for its welfare and beauty. In the neighborhood, our own personal sense of wholeness and joy is largely conditional upon that of the "other," whether friend or stranger. In this way, to be at home is to be at peace with our neighbors and the neighborhood, knowing there can be no real peace for any of us unless there is peace for all of us, and for all the places we share in common.

But in a world that has grown increasingly divided, polarized, even segregated by cultural, political, theological, and sociological distinctions, that sense of home seems ever more elusive. Whether we are living in a ramshackle tent on Sixth and San Pedro, or in an affluent gated community in the suburbs, or somewhere in between the two, our common context is one of chronic isolation that has led to a kind of spiritual homelessness. We are busy living our own lives, comfortably detached from one another, unaware that we need one another if we are ever to be most fully at home in the world.

We cope with this spiritual homelessness in one of two ways: indifference to the stranger, expressed in both unconscious and deliberate ways; or hostility toward the stranger, manifested both subtly and sometimes even blatantly. On the one hand, we either do not know or see the stranger on the sidewalk, let alone the neighbor next door; or, presuming that they are just another potential drain on our time, or resources, or energy, we may simply choose to ignore them.

On the other hand, because we do not know them, we may fear that they are a potential threat to us – to our safety, to our religious beliefs, to our ideals and values, to our way of life.

Such fear influences how we live our daily lives in the neighborhood. When we walk the streets among a crowd of strangers, we are constantly aware of where we keep our money; when we travel on an airplane, we are mindful of the ethnicity of those who are seated around us; when someone at the gas station asks us for a dollar, we are quick to make assumptions about their motives, their life choices, the credibility of their story. Rarely does the thought cross our mind that the kid wearing the hoodie on the neighborhood street, the woman seated next to us on the plane, the sad man with the outstretched hand at the gas station might be Christ himself, sent by God to save us from ourselves.

The consequence of this separation from one another is that everyone outside our tribe is a stranger whom, out of fear or indifference, we do not know. The middle-aged man from India who works five cubicles down from us on the third floor, the single mom whose fourth-grader plays shortstop on our son's Little League team, the teenager who bags our groceries at the super market, the old man who flips newspapers on our driveway each morning, the addict on the street—chances are we do not even know their names, let alone the aches and awes of their life stories. They can stand so near to us that we rub shoulders with them in the checkout line or on the subway, but even the physical proximity does not bridge the emotional, spiritual, psychic chasm that pervades our social experience and contributes to a climate of indifference and hostility. As Det. Graham Waters says in the movie *Crash*, "It's the sense of touch… nobody touches you. We're always behind this metal and glass. I think we miss that touch so much that we crash into each other, just so we can feel something." In other words, we simply do not know how to relate to each other peacefully in the neighborhoods in which we dwell.

But if we really want to *feel* something, then there are better alternatives than ignoring one another or crashing into one another. Only I do not believe the prescription we need calls for mere gestures of politeness, or terminal niceness, or so-called random acts of kindness, or even a greater adherence to the Golden Rule. The solution to the distance we feel between one another—the antidote to indifference and hostility—is not simply to *do* more, but to get out more, to see more, to listen more because, as Fredrick Buechner says,

> If we are to love our neighbors, before doing anything else we must see our neighbors. With our imagination as well as our eyes, that is to say like artists, we must see not just their faces but the life behind and within their faces.[1]

In the end, the cure to the indifference and hostility that separates us, and the finding of that home we are longing for, begins in the moment when the stranger becomes our neighbor—in the encounter when we finally know, and are finally known by, the "other." It begins in that moment when we confess our own indifference, conquer our fear of them and, like the incarnate Christ, dare to cross borders, swap stories, break bread, and stay a while with them. This, as you will see in the pages that follow, is Jesus' prescription for living a hospitable life in the neighborhood.

The day before we met Supreme at Sixth and San Pedro, we journeyed to Watts Towers in Los Angeles. Watts was the epicenter of violence both in the 1960's, during the Watts Riots, and in the 1990's, during the L.A. Uprising. While visiting the historic towers, a local resident of that community rolled in on his bicycle and struck up a conversation with a few of us. He shared passionately with us about his faith, his family, his pride for his revitalized community. When someone in our group shared with him that she had lived in Southern

California her entire life but had never before been to Watts, he shook his head and said, "Baby, you need to get out more."

His name was Levon, and his prophetic words were meant for all of us: we need to get out more.

This book is a call to action for those who desire to live a more hospitable life in a world of indifference and increasing hostility. It's for those who are willing to believe that the home we are searching for is not so much a home that is *found*, but one that is *formed* by intentional practices of Christian hospitality in the world. It assumes that the world is not nearly as hostile and inhospitable as we are led to believe, that there are angels out there, and that if we have any chance of encountering them at all, it will be along the neighborhood sidewalks, the city streets, the coffee houses, the local parks, and all the other ordinary places we pitch our daily tents.

This book is designed to provoke you to leave the house and make a home in the world—to coach you across the borders of indifference, suspicion, fear, and isolation on a voyage of discovery, adventure and, finally, neighborliness. You do not need to go to Sixth and San Pedro, or to Watts Towers, or to some distant or dangerous corner of your world in order to make this voyage. In fact, my suspicion is that you will not need to go very far at all, at least not at first. Getting out more might lead you to your next-door neighbor's front stoop, or to the local market, or to the coffeehouse on the corner. It might lead you to a soup kitchen for the hungry, or to an interfaith gathering, or to a City Council meeting. There, you will find plenty of strangers who, from God's perspective, are meant to be your neighbors.

My goal is to persuade you to consciously choose to live a more hospitable life in a world of strangers—to make hospitality your life's calling wherever you happen to be, and to pursue it daily in very practical, deeply personal ways. My goal is to motivate you to cross borders, swap stories, break bread, and abide with your neighbors, until the neighborhood starts to feel more like a home for all of us.

In the pages that follow, I'll challenge you to think about hospitality as any intentional act by which we extend God's generous welcome to the stranger. In Chapter One, we'll see how this unique understanding of hospitality represents a radical shift from how the world understands hospitality. Whereas our modern culture, driven by consumerist demands and the bottom line, defines hospitality as making people feel comfortable, indulged, even pampered, the Bible introduces us to a more selfless way of understanding hospitality that emphasizes a genuine desire to make the stranger feel known, loved, and welcomed—by us, and by God. Because this kind of hospitality does not come naturally to us, I suggest four essential practices that foster the hospitable life.

In Chapter Two, "Cross a Border," I propose the practice of crossing borders—not simply the physical borders that separate us from others, but also the borders of ideology, theology, culture, and worldview, to name just a few. Each of us lives with certain assumptions, biases, and beliefs about others, many of which simply are not true, and most of which we are not even aware because we do not get out enough. You can cross a border by going into the city or even by journeying across international lines. But you can also cross a border by talking with a neighbor three doors down whose beliefs or politics are fundamentally different from your own, or by relating to someone whose age, social class, life experience, or life needs are foreign to you. The truth about us is that, as is often said, "We don't know what we don't know." Every time we cross a border of some kind, we come to know a little more about ourselves and those with whom we share the sidewalk.

In Chapter Three, "Spin a Yarn," I propose the practice of sharing stories. We live in a culture that does not foster deep conversation between people. Ours is a generation of sound bites, small talk, bumper-sticker statements, elevator speeches, tweets and text messages under 140 characters. We talk at one another but we do not know how to talk *with* one another. So much of our public, political, and religious discourse conveys what we stand *for* and what we stand *against*. It's time that we find creative ways to talk about whom we stand *with*. By sharing our stories, we come to see our common humanity and the larger narrative of God's grace, which binds us together.

In Chapter Four, "Set the Table," I introduce the practice of sharing our bread with others. In every society and culture, the act of breaking bread with one another is the most universal symbol for welcome, acceptance, intimacy and solidarity. For Jesus, it became a symbol of God's boundless compassion, in this world and in the world to come. At the table of the Lord, those who were once strangers to God become children of God, and sisters and brothers to one another.

In Chapter Five, "Abide," I propose the practice of abiding or putting down deep and lasting roots in our communities. Too many people live with one finger on the eject button, all too eager to flee, unwilling to face the hard work of restoring our broken communities. In a culture that often seeks a quick savior to solve our biggest problems, those who desire to live more hospitably will put down roots in their neighborhoods and bloom where they are planted, putting their passions and gifts to work for the common good.

At the end of each chapter, I offer a handful of "Hospitality Apps" to help you apply these four practices to your daily life. Some of these applications may seem trivial, while others may seem a bit overwhelming. Pick and choose. Create your own. The apps I have suggested in this book are simply intended to expand your understanding of the specific practice, and to inspire you to "go and do" in your own unique context, based on your own unique gifts and talents.

I've tried to keep this book brief. There are plenty of scholars who have written on the subject of Christian hospitality with far greater depth and authority. My intention is not to be exhaustive or even scholarly on the subject of hospitality. If it were, I might have chosen as my title, "You Need to *Know* More." As it stands, my hope is that you'll come to learn just enough to want to get out more and practice the hospitable life today.

You need to get out more.

It will transform your life.

It will change your world.

It will lead you to that place called home, where you'll find all the other restless hearts of the world.

Let's go.

"Do not neglect to show hospitality to strangers, for by doing that some have entertained angels without knowing it."

—Hebrews 13:2

1

Hospitality Redux

THE FIRST TELEVISION SHOW I ever watched as a child was Mr. Rogers' Neighborhood. Every weekday, Mr. Rogers invited me into his home. He sang to me. He talked to me about important matters, like divorce, and going to the doctor, and how I shouldn't be afraid of being pulled down the bathtub drain because I couldn't possibly fit. I took him at his word because, over time, I had come to know him. We were neighbors.

Over the years, I came to know a lot about my neighbor, Mr. Rogers. I knew that each time he walked into his house, he'd take off his coat, hang it up in the closet, put on a zippered cardigan, and change from dress shoes into sneakers. I knew that he fed his gold fish faithfully. I knew that he treated his mail carrier, Mr. McFeely, with great kindness. Most of all, I knew that Mr. Rogers wanted me to be his neighbor, and that his neighborhood was safe. "It's such a good feeling," he sang, "a very good feeling, the feeling you know that we're friends."

Forty years later, I confess that I do not know my neighbors nearly as well. I don't even know the name of my mail carrier. This is not such a good, good feeling. I'm not so naïve to think that there must be a Neighborhood of Make-Believe out in the real world. I simply find myself wanting to know the real neighbors in my own community better—to know their stories, their needs, their hopes and dreams, and for them to know mine. I call them "neighbors," but in all honesty, I'm talking about strangers—whether they live three doors down from me, or three clicks down the road. It's a beautiful day in the neighborhood when these strangers become our friends.

The Challenge

After the Sept. 11 attacks more than ten years ago, Chief Rabbi Sir Jonathan Sacks of the United Hebrew Congregations of the Commonwealth said,

> I used to think that the greatest commandment in the Bible was 'You shall love your neighbor as yourself.' I was wrong. Only in one place does the Bible ask us to love our neighbor. In more than thirty places it commands us to love the stranger...It isn't hard to love our neighbors because by and large our neighbors are like us. What's tough is to love the stranger, the person who isn't like us, who has a different skin color, or a different faith, or a different background. That's the real challenge. It was in ancient times. It still is today.[2]

"I've always wanted to have a neighbor just like you," sang Mr. Rogers. "I've always wanted to live in a neighborhood with you." I think what Mr. Rogers understood about his neighborhood was that neighborhoods are made one neighbor at a time; that until you ask someone, "Won't you be my neighbor," they'll forever remain strangers to you.

Getting it Right

The biblical practice of making neighbors is called *hospitality*, a word that the secular world has, in more recent years, claimed and practiced more ardently than many modern Christians, even as it has exploited its original meaning. The very mention of the word hospitality these days calls to mind an entire industry that has dedicated itself to making guests and travelers feel, as they say, "right at home." To that end, our favorite hotel leaves a freshly baked chocolate chip cookie on our pillow; the bed and breakfast appoints freshly cut flowers on our nightstand; the cruise ship assigns to us a personal porter to respond to our every self-indulgent request. In the secular, commercial world, hospitality is synonymous with customer service, with pampering and small indulgences, with an expression of warmth that is not so much genuine as it is expeditious and profitable.

Even in the church, our attempts at showing hospitality to visitors tend most often to be somewhat self-serving. When visitors arrive, we want them to like us, and we especially want them to come back. Our hospitality teams measure their effectiveness by how well they greet people at the door, or how fresh the fair trade coffee happens to be at the fellowship hour, or by the quality of the informational brochure we stuff into the hands of our first-time visitors. These are all necessary and effective ways to welcome people, but they are not the fullest expression of Christian hospitality because they are passive by nature—that is to say, they seek to welcome the stranger *only* when the stranger has arrived and, in the end, their primary objective is to make the stranger one of us.

This way of practicing hospitality is modeled on the commands of Hebrew Scriptures to welcome the stranger. There are at least 36 such commands in the Old Testament, all of which obligate us to welcome the sojourner among us because, as Deuteronomy reminds us, we ourselves were once sojourners in Egypt. In other words, welcoming the stranger is an act of remembering our past—that we were once strangers in a strange, inhospitable land, in desperate need of the generosity and neighborliness of others. The New Testament, and in particular the Letter to the Hebrews, carries this mandate even further, suggesting that we are to welcome the sojourner who knocks on our door: "Keep on loving each other as brothers, and do not forget to entertain strangers, for by doing so some people have entertained angels without knowing it" (13:1-2). One translation, *The Message*, puts the command in more simple terms: "Be ready with a meal or a bed when it's needed."

It all makes rational sense, and yet what we have is a biblical theology of hospitality that adopts a passive posture. We wait for the stranger to appear. We are off the hook until we hear the knock on our door. The command is not to get out and actively seek out the stranger, but to wait for him to arrive. Until then, the stranger is still very much a stranger to us.

This is how we have historically understood hospitality anyway. But the New Testament word for hospitality, I believe, is our key for redefining our call to live more hospitable lives. In the biblical Greek, the particular word for hospitality is *philoxenia*, but if you happen to be a little rusty with your Greek, perhaps the best way to grasp the true meaning of *philoxenia* is to consider its more familiar antonym, which we know as *xenophobia*, or "fear of the stranger." For the early Christians, the practice of hospitality, or philoxenia, meant more than merely extending courtesy or generosity to the sojourner; it meant, quite literally, loving the stranger, even to point of actively, passionately pursuing the stranger.

For the early church, hospitality required Christians to get out from under their beds and enter a world that was fiercely hostile to the gospel and its adherents. It meant leaving the safe bunker of the church community and, at great risk, seeking out the outcast, the neglected, the most vulnerable, the sinners and the sojourners who wandered among them without a place to call home. And for those early Christians who had everything to fear—whose own fragile community faced the constant threat of persecution and extinction under the heavy heel of the Empire—hospitality, or love of the stranger, became the antidote to their xenophobia. More than any other outward Christian practice, hospitality became the primary means by which the church grew in numbers. And more than any other biblical injunction, the parable of "The Judgment of the Nations," from Matthew 25:31-46, served as their guide:

> When the Son of Man comes in his glory, and all the
> angels with him, then he will sit on the throne of his

glory. All the nations will be gathered before him, and he will separate people one from another as a shepherd separates the sheep from the goats, and he will put the sheep at his right hand and the goats at the left. Then the king will say to those at his right hand, "Come, you that are blessed by my Father, inherit the kingdom prepared for you from the foundation of the world; for I was hungry and you gave me food, I was thirsty and you gave me something to drink, I was a stranger and you welcomed me, I was naked and you gave me clothing, I was sick and you took care of me, I was in prison and you visited me." Then the righteous will answer him, "Lord, when was it that we saw you hungry and gave you food, or thirsty and gave you something to drink? And when was it that we saw you a stranger and welcomed you, or naked and gave you clothing? And when was it that we saw you sick or in prison and visited you?" And the king will answer them, "Truly I tell you, just as you did it to one of the least of these who are members of my family, you did it to me." Then he will say to those at his left hand, "You that are accursed, depart from me into the eternal fire prepared for the devil and his angels; for I was hungry and you gave me no food, I was thirsty and you gave me nothing to drink, I was a stranger and you did not welcome me, naked and you did not give me clothing, sick and in prison and you did not visit me." Then they also will answer, "Lord, when was it that we saw you hungry or thirsty or a stranger or naked or sick or in prison, and did not take care of you?" Then he will answer them, "Truly I tell you, just as you did not do it to one of the least of these, you did not do it to me."

According to historians, in the period following the Apostolic Age, Christians committed themselves to a movement of exuberant caring and hospitality that was unique in all of antiquity. Julian the Apostate, a fierce enemy of Christianity, lamented that 'the godless Galileans (Christians) fed not only their poor but ours also." In other words, by their love of and care for the stranger, Christians slowly converted the pagan world. By the middle of the third century, early church historians noted that the Christian community was caring for some 1,500 ordinary citizens of Rome, seeking them out, bringing them in, restoring them to health and wholeness. In the end, it wasn't their dynamic and entertaining worship services, or their innovative evangelism strategies, or even their charismatic preachers that primarily grew the early Church. It was, quite simply, their shared commitment to the hospitable life, embodied in the practices of loving the stranger.

If there is one practice that the world desperately needs and that Christians urgently need to reclaim, it is this ancient practice of Christian hospitality. Our modern lives are growing increasingly more isolated and tribal; our fear of the stranger is growing ever more palpable; our churches are growing more and more detached and insulated from the neighbors around them.   It is no wonder, then, that the world is growing increasingly more inhospitable.

Stranger Danger

For more than two decades, futurist Faith Popcorn, an authoritative voice on consumer trends in the United States, has carefully tracked what she describes as the trend of "cocooning."[3] In the early 1990's, Popcorn predicted that Americans would gradually retreat to the safety of their personal homes, seeking to insulate themselves from any normal social involvement that might be perceived as unfriendly, dangerous, or otherwise threatening. "Home sweet home," predicted Popcorn, would more accurately be defined in the 21st century as "Home safe home."

Popcorn suggested that advances in technology would make cocooning even easier and more attractive for Americans. Long before the days of Amazon.com and eBay, Popcorn predicted the day when, instead of venturing out and shopping at the mall or supermarket, we would make our purchases online, from the privacy and safety of our home. Instead of going to the movie theater, we would build elaborate entertainment systems called "home theaters" and, without even leaving the house, we would rent our movies, which would arrive in the mail the next day. Popcorn suggested that, because violence in the work place is the fastest growing type of violence in the US, Americans would find ways to work from home offices. Because school safety is a growing concern for our children, more Americans would turn to home schooling, and more and more college students would seek online degrees. Because local parks and restaurants in most major cities are surrounded geographically by crime and violence, Americans would turn to their own gardens to burrow in and live green, and fashion their own gourmet kitchens for healthy, organic dining.

The trend is called "cocooning." The mantra is "better safe than sorry." The root cause is grounded in our chronic fear of the stranger, and the consequence is that we are living progressively isolated, self-absorbed, socially detached lives.

The late Henri Nouwen noted that the greatest obstacle to practicing hospitality in our lives is the crippling hostility that pervades every aspect of the American way of life. Nouwen suggested that, not only do we fear that some people are out to do us harm, but we suspect that there are others who are out to use us for their own personal gain, and others who are out to get what we have or what we want for ourselves, and still others whose own set of beliefs somehow make us feel threatened or insecure about what we ourselves believe. We live in a culture of hostility, rooted in competition, rivalry, greed, suspicion, fear and even aggression. It creeps into our religion, our politics, our vocations, our relationships with others and with other nations, even our families. And that pervasive hostility often makes any expression of Christian hospitality seem not only irrational and inconvenient, but dangerous.[4]

Unless, of course, we can understand hospitality, not merely as a function of doing, but as a way of embodying God's welcome in the world by moving toward others with a posture that fosters acceptance, neighborliness, and generosity. A hospitable life creates space in the world where the stranger in our midst can become a neighbor. It is less concerned with changing people, or bringing them over to our side, or converting them to our way, on our terms, in order to make them more safe to us. It's more concerned with seeking opportunities for us to find God most fully alive in *them*, and to befriend *that* part of them above all else—above our own agendas, our own needs, our fears, hostilities, judgments and assumptions.

Lose Your Illusion

The hostility that pervades our common life in the neighborhood is often more imagined than it is real. The world is not as uninhabitable, inhospitable as we are sometimes led to believe. A colleague shared about an experience she had one dark, late evening while on a business trip in a major city. She had just left a meeting and was walking alone to her car in an empty, unlit parking lot when, once inside, she tried to start her car, only to discover that her battery was dead. She is one of those rare people who, at the time, did not believe in carrying a cell phone. So there she was, with a car that would not start, in an unlit parking lot, with no means of calling for help and no idea of what to do next.

All kinds of thoughts ran through her mind—I am alone, it's midnight, I am a woman, I am stranded, and on and on and on… She then noticed a dark car driving slowly through the parking lot, lurking, prowling in her general direction. She checked and rechecked the locks on the doors. She tried, over and over again, to start her car as the strange car's headlights slowly approached. Her hands began to tremble; her heart pounded; terrifying thoughts ran through her mind as the car drew nearer and came to a stop in front of hers. As the two dark figures emerged, she tried, in vain, to start the engine. The men walked back to the trunk of their car, removing what appeared to her in the dark to be a thick rope. They walked slowly toward her car, one on each side. Nearly in tears, full of fear and panic, she was ready to throw both hands on the horn, when one of the men knocked bluntly on her windshield, held up a pair of jumper cables and said, "You don't have to get out of your car, lady. Just open the hood for us and we'll try to get it started for you."

Maybe much of the hostility that both surrounds us and dwells within us is real and true. But maybe, too, it's often the simple thought of it—the imagined possibility of it—that keeps us from living hospitable lives.

The early church wrote the prescription that can cure our modern illness of cocooning and the fear that pervades our social experience. It's called philoxenia—the intentional practice of getting out, of actively pursuing the strangers among us, of meeting them where they are, loving them where they're at, and walking with them into the household of God. Philoxenia assumes that this "household" has a roof so wide that it stretches far beyond the boundaries of race, class, politics, religion or any other limited social construct, which is perhaps the best news of all, because the goal of hospitality is not necessarily to bring the stranger into our familiar world, but to get out of our world and meet them in their own.

Leave the Bunker

Consider the story of Homeboy Industries near China Town in Los Angeles. Founded by Father Gregory Boyle in 1992, Homeboy Industries provides an empowering alternative to inner city violence for hundreds of former gang members— many of whom have been recently released from prison. At Homeboy Industries, these men and women are offered counseling and recovery groups, a tattoo-removal service, job training and placement, and on-site employment at Homeboy Silkscreen, Homeboy Bakery, Homeboy Merchandising, and Homegirl Cafe. You can read of Father Boyle's extraordinary work in his memoir, *Tattoos on the Heart*.

One of the most compelling aspects of Boyle's ministry is how it all began when, in 1986, he was appointed by his Diocese to serve a small Latino congregation in Boyle Heights. Almost immediately, Boyle began riding his bike nightly through the gang-plagued housing projects of Aliso Gardens; and on those nightly bike rides, he would befriend the homies who lived there. They eventually came to know him as "G," or "Father G," or just "G-Dawg." On several occasions, Boyle found himself unwittingly riding his bike into the middle of a gunfight between rival gang members, and each time the homies would tackle him to the ground and shield him from the bullets. Despite the risks and imminent threats of danger, Boyle was undeterred and, over time, his ministry of boundless compassion eventually transformed that community.

Today, Homeboy Industries and its many programs are so well known among the projects of Los Angeles that Boyle no longer needs to ride his bike into the middle of gunfights. He employs more than 700 homies who come to him when they are finally ready to make a change and lay down their weapons, and there are so many of them now that Boyle cannot take them all in. Even still, his ministry of hospitality has saved the lives of thousands of men and women, and promises to save thousands more.

Boyle's well-ridden bike is now retired and sits on permanent display in a local museum—a timeless symbol, a holy relic of a man who dared to ride into the hostile neighborhoods of complete strangers, and refused to ride out until he could call them friends. His unique vision calls to mind the opening scene of the Gospel of John, in which we are given the purest image of hospitality in all of Scripture. It says, "In the beginning was the Word, and the Word was with God, and the Word was God." At a particular time in human history, "that Word became flesh, and entered the neighborhood." (John 1:14). That "Word" is God himself, in the person of Jesus Christ, who came to us as a complete stranger, and would not leave until he could call us friends.

If you could take a ride on Father Boyle's bike, where would it take you?

Perhaps it's asking too much of us to ride into a gunfight among enemies in the name of hospitality, but I believe there are faithful alternatives, and I believe the place to start is by confronting our own debilitating, often irrational fears of the strangers among us, or at least our general indifference to them. Perhaps we can begin by moving toward the people we are apt to see every day, yet who still remain strangers to us.   As Margot Starbuck suggests in her book, *Small Things with Great Love*, people who seek to do so will pattern their lives after Jesus, who was not so much moved by courage, but by love.

> When we are no longer driven by self-preservation, Jesus moves in and through us to engage with others across natural barriers. What this means is that our lives—at work, at home, at school—start to look more like his. Instead of backing away from the kind of needy ones who can make the rest of us so uncomfortable—the deaf, the blind, the sick, the lepers, the demon-possessed—we make a point, like Jesus did, of moving toward them. At church, we step toward the brother in personal crisis. In our neighborhoods, we

embrace the single mom struggling to feed and clothe her children. In our communities, we respond with assistance to a report in the local paper about the ones nearby whose home burned down.[5]

Driven by Love

We live in a culture that reduces the misfortune of others to must-see TV. From Judge Judy to Dr. Phil, from Ricki Lake to Jerry Springer, from high-speed car chases on the evening news to the sensationalized funerals of fallen pop icons, our culture has a strange love affair with the casual, discreet observation of tragedy and hard luck and human sin. As Bono of U2 once sang, "I can't tell the difference between ABC News and Hill Street Blues." It's all so terribly entertaining. Call it social voyeurism.

The real life people with real human needs we see every day can so easily become for us just stories, dramas, played out by mere actors or subjects on a stage. Consider the telling scene in the movie, *Patch Adams*:

> PROFESSOR: "Here we have a juvenile onset diabetic with poor circulation and diabetic neuropathy. As you can see, these are diabetic ulcers with lymphedema and evidence of gangrene. Questions?"
>
> STUDENT 1: "Any osteomyelitis?"
>
> PROFESSOR: (As he looks at medical chart) "None apparent, although not definitive."
>
> STUDENT 2: "Treatment?"
>
> PROFESSOR: "To stabilize the blood sugar, consider antibiotics, possibly amputation." (Patient gasps and pulls the bed sheets tightly around her neck).

PATCH: (from the back of the group) "What's her name? I was just wondering the patient's name."

PROFESSOR: (glancing at the chart) "Marjorie."

PATCH: "Hi, Marjorie."

MARJORIE: (with a big smile) "Hi."

PROFESSOR: (clearing his throat) "Yes, uh, thank you. Let's move on."

The longest journey we will ever take in our lives is the journey from the head to the heart, where what we see and hear and think about the stranger is humanized in the form of genuine empathy. Here in the heart, the stranger becomes our equal.

The second longest journey, and the most important journey of all, is from the heart to the gut, where our sympathy is surpassed by an unmistakable sense of compassionate responsibility to the stranger. Here, at the gut level, we know we must do something. This is the hospitable moment most pregnant with opportunity.

The Greek verb in the New Testament for "having compassion" is *splagchnizomai*. *Splagchnizomai* is rooted in another Greek word that means "entrails" (our vital, internal organs). When, for example, Jesus encounters 5,000 hungry people with no one to feed them, he is "overcome with compassion" (Matthew 14:14). It's not an intellectual response; nor is it even an emotional or sentimental response. What he feels is visceral—something felt deep inside, at the gut level, which cannot be subjugated. Jesus knows he must do something. And he does.

The pathway to a more hospitable life leads us from our casual, distant observation of the stranger's plight to a genuine empathy by which we see the stranger as an equal, until finally we are overcome by a deep-seated, gut-wrenching love that compels us to do something for them.

The Goal is Soul

The hospitable life is, in other words, a deeply "incarnational" journey into the neighborhood that is fueled by God's unwavering love and concern for those who are near to us, and those who are unknown to us. It is not "terminal niceness," as theologian Letty Russell maintains, where the host attempts to make the guest more comfortable or at home. It is not limited to welcoming people who share our own class, race, gender, political positions or religious convictions. It's not swooping into the problems of others as if we had the solutions, nor is it charity, or handouts or global or local missions. Absent of self-superiority, the hospitable life is one that enters into the world of others as a guest and, in a spirit of mutuality, shares equally in the unfolding, transformative promises offered by God in each unique encounter. Just as God's love for the world drove Jesus into our neighborhood to be with us and for us, this same love drives each of us from our isolation and fear to be with and for those whom God loves.

Rick King, a low-budget movie director, had found himself in the depths of despair over his career, which was going nowhere fast. Angry, depressed, and bitter, he took his eight-year old twins to the Santa Monica pier with a friend for a walk along the beach. They had just spent a glorious morning surfing and were surrounded by beach gear, when King heard a garbled voice and looked over to see a man with a twisted face in a wheelchair. King writes,

> He was talking to me but I couldn't understand a word he said. Obviously he had some kind of physical problem. He repeated himself and I started to adjust to his speech pattern. "Excuse me," he was saying, "Can you help me?"
>
> Does it ever end? I thought to myself. Can you live in Santa Monica and not be approached for just one day? I was put off by his slurred speech and facial

contortions.   Immediately, he picked up on my discomfort. "I don't bite," he said.

"What do you need," I asked, ready to dig into my pocket for change.

"Could you help me go to the bathroom," he asked.

Suddenly I wanted to be fixing the Mir space station. The men's public restroom at the beach is one of the most unpleasant I've ever been in.

I clutched at the chance my ears had deceived me. "What do you need?" I repeated. But he was very firm and not in the least shy. "Could you help me go to the bathroom?"

OK, I replied, ashamed to reply otherwise. I figured he just needed some help getting in the door.

We headed in that direction and chatted. His name was Neal and he has cerebral palsy. Then we got to the door and I offered to help him maneuver through. But he was quite dismissive. That wasn't the help he needed. He insisted that I go in first.

With a sinking feeling, I went in. It was obvious I was nervous but Neal took over the situation like a good director, giving clear and concise instructions that began with: "Unzip my fly."

Well here we are in a public bathroom and I'm unzipping a man's fly, I thought. The process was intimate and involved my holding a plastic cup. "It'll take a couple of minutes," he informed me. So, while I held the cup, we talked.

He lives in the Valley. His attendant had driven him to the beach and left him there for a couple of hours. "I'm very independent," Neal said proudly. He was curious about my work. I explained about making films and he told me he hadn't seen a movie in 20 years. "Too expensive. But I watch a lot of television." "Well, you can see my movies there," I replied. "If they make the theaters, they don't usually stay there long." And suddenly I didn't feel so bad about it.

After a couple of minutes, I washed the cup and put it back in the bag behind his chair. I offered to help push Neal out of the bathroom but he didn't want any help that he didn't need. We got out into the brilliant sunshine as buff dudes and pretty girls skated past. We said goodbye and I watched the wheelchair disappear into the crowd.

"That was very nice of you to do that," one of the boys told me. I brushed it off. "What was I going to do? Say no?" But in my mind, I was thinking it was very nice of Neal to let me help him.[6]

Whenever genuine Christian hospitality is practiced, the lines between host and guest are blurred, walls of fear and indifference are broken down, and grace flows in—not just into one life, but two.

At a particular time in human history, "the Word became flesh, and entered the neighborhood." To those who let him in, he says, "Go and do likewise."

Prayer—

> We saw a stranger yesterday.
> We put food in the eating place,
> Drink in the drinking place,
> Music in the listening place,
> And with the sacred name of the triune God
> He blessed us and our house,
> Our cattle and our dear ones.
> As the lark says in her song:
> Often, often, often, goes the Christ
> In the stranger's guise.

True evangelical faith
cannot lie dormant
it clothes the naked
it feeds the hungry
it comforts the sorrowful
it shelters the destitute
it serves those that harm it
it binds up that which is wounded
it has become all things to all creatures.

—Menno Simmons, 16th century[7]

Hospitality Apps

Adventures in the Neighborhood

1. Speak to the next stranger you come across. As Julien
    Smith, in *The Flinch*, suggests: "Whether he looks
    interesting or not, whether you are attracted to or
    repelled by him, or whether you can think of anything
    to say—none of these things matter. Strike up a
    conversation, even if it's just for 15 seconds. Look the
    person in the eye as you do so. Smile. Do this to test
    your ability to force yourself through discomfort. As
    you perform this exercise, one of two things will
    happen. First, you may just start a conversation
    quickly. "Excuse me, which direction is this subway
    going?" You'll notice that the faster you do this, the
    easier it is."[8]

2. Say yes to what's next. We talk ourselves out of too
    much. We fashion excuses for why we need to stay
    home. We back out of too many opportunities to get
    to know our neighbors. Practice saying yes. Say yes to
    the next request that comes your way:

    -   A colleague at work whom you do not know well
        asks you to lunch, or to her Christmas party, or to a
        baseball game—say yes.

    -   Someone on the corner asks if you can spare a
        dollar—say yes.

    -   The blood bank calls and asks if you can spare a
        pint—say yes.

    -   A neighbor knocks on your door and invites to you
        to his backyard barbeque—say yes.

3. Find a partner. The hospitable life is fostered in
    ongoing partnership with others. Jesus sent his
    disciples out two-by-two for several reasons: (a) for
    accountability—we need others to help us stay focused

on our mission, to test our assumptions and biases, to check our egos and our motivations, and to keep us in the game when we are fearful; (b) for sustainability— because engaging a world of need can often be physically exhausting and emotionally draining, having someone stand with us and work alongside us is not only empowering and heartening, but is often the cure to compassion fatigue; (c) diversity—because some people have gifts and talents that we do not possess, we are stronger and more effective when, as the Apostle Paul says, "all the parts of the body work together." We need one another, just as a body needs all of its parts.

Moses had Aaron. Mary had Elizabeth. Jesus had twelve disciples, but Peter and James and John were his closest partners in ministry. Paul had Timothy and Titus. David had Jonathan. Ruth had Naomi.

You need to get out more but, like the disciples of Jesus, you don't need to go alone. You need to take someone with you. Find a partner and:

- Volunteer at a local soup kitchen, assisted living center, or food bank.

- Attend a city council meeting to learn about local issues.

- Bring coffee or a breakfast burrito to the local "jornaleros" or day laborers who gather on the corner near the home improvement stores in your community.

- Take a tour of the resource centers in your community that serve the poor and those in need.

- Join or start a "meet up" group at www.meetup.com, where hundreds, even thousands of people in your community come together every day around affinities, interests, or causes (like Asperger's, wine tasting, hiking, and vegetarianism) to "Do something, Learn something, Share something, Change something."

"The supreme religious challenge is to see God's image in one
who is not in our image."

—Rabbi Jonathan Sacks

2

Cross a Border

YOU NEED TO GET OUT MORE. Whether you are mindful of it or not, you live with certain assumptions, biases, and beliefs about others, many of which simply are not true, and some of which may keep you too close to home. These assumptions and predispositions function in your life as invisible borders, separating you from those whose beliefs or politics or ethnicity may be fundamentally different from your own, or whose age, social class, life experience, or life needs are foreign to you. The truth about us is that, as is often said, "We don't know what we don't know." Every time we get out and cross one of these borders, we come to know a little more about ourselves and those with whom we share the sidewalk.

In Robert Frost's poem, "Mending Wall," two neighbors meet one day in the springtime out in the fields, at the stone wall that separates their two farms. As they walk along the wall together, each on their own side, they begin to replace the stones that had fallen during the harsh winter.

His neighbor believes in the necessity of the wall. "Good fences," he says, "make good neighbors." But the poet has his doubts. He protests,

> Something there is that doesn't love a wall,
> That sends the frozen-ground-swell under it,
> And spills the upper boulder in the sun,
> And makes gaps even two can pass abreast.

As the two neighbors, each on their own side, wear their fingers rough, handling the stones, rebuilding the wall, the poet comes to see the futility of their work. He knows that only those who have cows have need of a fence, and because neither of them have cows, he concludes that there's really nothing to be kept in or kept out by the wall—except, of course, each other. He thinks to himself,

> Before I built a wall I'd ask to know
> What I was walling in or walling out,
> And to whom I was like to give offense.
> Something there is that doesn't love a wall,
> That wants it down…

The world is full of walls. Everywhere we go, there are fences, gates, partitions and other cleverly constructed barriers—all intended to keep something or someone in, and to prevent something or someone else from getting in. Walls define the boundaries of what belongs to us, and what does not belong to others. Walls define our sovereignty and security as individuals, even as nations. Walls often serve a useful purpose.

Invisible Walls

Beyond the physical walls that demarcate the boundaries of property and space, there are other, more insidious walls that we are apt to live behind. These are the less visible, highly portable walls that define the boundaries of our relationships with our neighbors and the limits of our responsibility to them. And these walls are everywhere. They are the walls of culture and class and race, of politics and religion and nationality and ancestry. They separate the rich from the poor, the Republican from the Democrat, liberals from conservatives, blue collar from white collar. They separate those who live in the inner city from those in the suburbs, Israelis from Palestinians, Irish Catholics from Protestants, evangelicals from mainliners, the Hatfields from the McCoys, Christians from Muslims, from Jews, and from atheists.

We build these walls and rebuild them over the course of our lives in an effort to define who we are and who we are not, what we believe and do not believe, what we stand for and what we cannot tolerate, who is our neighbor and who is not our neighbor. These walls become so much a part of our lives that we do not even see them anymore. They become, over time, an acceptable, assumed part of our reality and how we see the world.

It's said that it only takes about three weeks to become blind to the presence of stationary objects in our everyday worlds. Hang a new picture on the wall, and you're likely to notice it for about 21 days. After that it just becomes part of the scenery. It no longer leaps into the foreground. It's your new reality.

As Christoff says in the movie *The Truman Show*, "We accept the reality with which we are presented." So many of these walls become our accepted reality, and then we pass that reality down to our children and grandchildren, who commit to maintaining those same walls, some of which we have built ourselves, many of which we've inherited from *our* ancestors. And the next generation maintains those same walls, sometimes with hands worn rough and hearts as hardened as the stones they carry. And soon enough you will hear them say, "My grandfather never liked those people, my father never liked those people, and I will never like those people. It's just in my blood." They'll say, "I was raised to believe this or to believe that, and good or bad, I'll never believe otherwise."

And so the poet, gazing over the stone wall, says of his neighbor,

He will not go behind his father's saying,

And he likes having thought of it so well.

He says it again, "Good fences make good neighbors.[9]

Hospitable Heretics

George Bernard Shaw noted, "All great truths begin as blasphemies." Behind every wall, beyond every border is a truth awaiting your discovery. Pursue it, and it will challenge your own understanding of truth. It will expand the boundaries of your neighborhood. It will disrupt the status quo. It will likely make you a heretic.

A friend of mine was talking with his daughter one evening over dinner. She had just come home from college for the holidays, and at some point in the conversation she confessed that she had been struggling with something. She had attended a Bible study in the college dormitory with some students down the hall. They had read the passage in the Gospel of John in which Jesus says, "I am the way, and the truth, and the life." She told her father, "I had always liked that little verse—until the Bible study leader told us what he thought that it meant."

"And what did he say that it means," asked the father?

"Well," she said, "he insisted it means that, unless you're a Christian, there's no way to God—that unless you believe in Jesus, you're lost, and you will not go to heaven."

The father could see that his daughter was troubled. He said, "Is that what you believe?"

"I think a lot of Christians believe that," she said, "but I don't. My roommate is a Buddhist, from Korea, and she's one of the kindest people I know. And the beautiful woman who works in the cafeteria—she has that red dot on her forehead—she's Hindu. My Calculus professor is Muslim, and he prays more than anyone I have ever known. I believe God loves them and would never reject them."

Her father said, "So, if this what you believe, then why are you struggling?"

She said, "I'm struggling because, if this is what I believe, then can I still call myself a Christian?"

Her father replied, "Unless that's what you *do* believe, I don't see how you *can* be a Christian."

What about Them?

How do we relate to people of other faith traditions, cultures, nations? How does God relate to people whose faith is not distinctively Christian? It's a question that has needled Christians since the formation of the early church. What about those who live on the other side of the wall? If they're not one of us, are they still one of God's own?

Historically speaking, Christians have failed miserably in answering such questions. From the Crusades to the Holocaust, from the medieval Inquisitions of Europe to the witch trials of the American Colonies to the widespread religious intolerance of the post 9/11 world, the question has echoed down the halls of history: what about *them*?

It's a question that speaks not only to the deep *religious* divisions of our world, but to the larger ideological, cultural and political differences that divide humanity as a whole.

On July 22, 2011, Anders Breivik went on a shooting and bombing rampage in Norway, killing 77 people. He claimed that his actions were a necessary response to an increasingly multicultural, pluralistic society that was overly hospitable to Muslims, in particular, and which threatened the ethnically and religiously homogenous nation of Norway. His own people, he suggested, were losing their rightful place in their native land.

Weeks after that tragedy, here in the US, we commemorated the tenth anniversary of the September 11 terrorist attacks. We remembered how, in the midst of our personal and national

grief at that time, we overcame every cultural, religious, political
and social boundary imaginable to unite around the themes of
compassion, neighborliness, and commitment to our common
fragile humanity. In the days following the attacks, Muslims
and Jews and Hindus and Christians lit candles and held vigil
with one another. Democrats and Republicans who had once
avoided each other like the plague instinctively worked side-by-
side in a spirit of cooperation. People of every tribe and race
and class found common ground in their grief and in their
resilience. Nations from every corner of the globe pledged
their solidarity and unity.

When so much of our world had been turned upside down,
a conversation began in just about every civic and religious and
personal arena, about how our lives had changed, and would
continue to change, in the days and years that followed. While
we were many and diverse, we were one human family. We
would move on, but only if we moved on together, and moved
toward one another.

We then invaded two countries, in the name of securing our
borders.

Jesus the Trespasser

Jesus never built a wall. He never stayed put. He was always
on the move. Time and time again in the gospels, Jesus is
crossing borders, scaling walls, and blurring boundaries as he
moves toward the stranger. He is *El Buen Coyote*, as Bob
Ekblad calls him,[10] crossing borders, breaking the law,
smuggling people into the Kingdom of God, free of charge.
He carries the blind across the borders of the sightless and the
poor across the borders of invisibility. He smuggles the sin-
sick across the borders of religious law and moral justice into
the wide-open land of grace and forgiveness. He carries
outcast lepers through the city gates and restores them to their
communities. He raises the dead and the good-as-dead across

the borders of tombstone and time-hardened traditions, restoring them to life. Jesus never meets a border he is not willing to cross—whether that of geography, culture, ethnicity, religion, social class, or even the thin border that separates this life from the life eternal.

On one occasion, Jesus is on a road trip, traveling through gentile territory, when he's approached by a desperate woman from Canaan whose daughter has fallen ill. The daughter's condition is so grim that the mother resorts to begging this traveling Jewish healer from Nazareth to come to her rescue. "Jesus," she pleads from her knees, "have mercy. Help us" (Matthew 15).

But Matthew reports that Jesus is surprisingly reluctant to comply. They could not be any more different from each other. She is a woman, he a man. She is a Gentile, he a Jew. She worship idols, he is a monotheist. She speaks a different language, has a different skin color, comes from a different tribe. "Jesus, Son of David, have mercy," she cries out.

Jesus' response to the woman seems altogether un-Christian, but this is because he wants us to overhear him. Jesus, in this story, speaks for us:

> But he did not answer her at all. And his disciples came and urged him, saying, 'Send her away, for she keeps shouting after us.' He answered, 'I was sent only to the lost sheep of the house of Israel.' But she came and knelt before him, saying, 'Lord, help me.' He answered, 'It is not fair to take the children's food and throw it to the dogs.' She said, 'Yes, Lord, yet even the dogs eat the crumbs that fall from their masters' table.' Then Jesus answered her, 'Woman, great is your faith! Let it be done for you as you wish.' And her daughter was healed instantly (Matthew 15:23-28).

Some have suggested that this story proves that even Jesus
has serious trouble crossing the age-old religious and
ideological boundaries of his Hebrew tradition. Others suggest
that this bold woman from Canaan was essential to Jesus' own
conversion to a more inclusive religious posture—that even
Jesus needed a little push out of his comfort zone.

But let's be honest. We know enough about Jesus in the
gospels to conclude that it's not Jesus who has the problem
here.

It's his disciples. It's the early readers of this story. And it's
us.

In the story, Jesus speaks for us. Jesus plays the part of
antagonist on our behalf so that we can see ourselves in the
story. He recites our familiar litany of assumptions and
excuses, so that every unreasonable pretext for why we cannot
help a stranger from the other side of the border is neutralized,
so that the stranger is humanized, so that we come to see what
it actually looks like when someone crosses over one of those
archaic divisions in this world and dares to act on the belief that
there is no one who lives outside the love and concern of God.

Jesus, *El Buen Coyote*, carries us across the borders of apathy
and narrow-mindedness into the expansive Kingdom of
welcome and embrace. Out of compassion, in a spirit of
radical inclusion, the outsider is brought inside the care and
concern of God. This happens only because the insider named
Jesus ventures outside—out from behind the false dichotomies
that we would construct for him in order to keep him to
ourselves, so that the care and concern of God can be brought
to those who have not known it, and who may not even
acknowledge it.

God on the Loose

Border crossing is not as heretical as you may have been led to
believe. One of the tenets of orthodox Christian theology—

one of the central pillars of our tradition—is the doctrine of the "sovereignty of God." It's a concept that is outlined in Methodism's very first *General Article of Religion*, and it's central to all mainline Protestant statements of faith. For United Methodists, it reads this way:

> There is one living and true God, everlasting, without body or parts, of infinite power, wisdom, and goodness; the maker and preserver of all things, both visible and invisible.[11]

What it means is that, if God really is God, then God's infinite power, wisdom and goodness have no limits or boundaries. God is on the loose, unrestrained by human borders and boundaries. If God chooses to speak through a religious tradition other than our own, then God is free to do so. If God chooses to speak through a golden sunset, or through the laws of quantum physics, or through the music of Bob Dylan or BB King or Beethoven, God is free to do so, because God is God. The mysteries of God cannot be contained in any of our systems of belief. God is larger than our imaginations, our experiences, our theological systems. God's care and concern for all creation spill out beyond our walls, seep through our borders, and blur the boundaries of our world.

Don McCullough, an evangelical Christian, describes it this way:

> A child at the beach digs a hole in the sand and, with her little bucket, busily sets about transferring the ocean into it. We smile at the grandeur of her ambition, but only because we know she will soon mature beyond such pathetic futility. An ocean cannot be contained in any hole of any size on any continent. And neither can God be fully contained within any theological system.[12]

Paul the Un-Builder

If this is a growing edge for you—this idea that God is bigger
than the systems and doctrines we create to contain God—then
the story of the Apostle Paul will prove instructive and
liberating. Near the end of his life, while in prison, Paul wrote
a letter to the church in Ephesus, reminding the gentile
converts to never forget that there was a time in their lives
when they had no hope—when they were far off from God,
unreachable, lost—until Jesus crossed the borders of religion,
race and nationality to find them. Now, writes Paul, these same
gentiles are one with the Jews. There are no distinctions
between them. Jesus has broken down the dividing wall,

> …so that he might create in himself one new humanity
> in place of the two, thus making peace, and might
> reconcile both groups to God in one body through the
> cross, thus putting to death that hostility through it. So
> he came and proclaimed peace to you who were far off
> and peace to those who were near; for through him
> both of us have access in one Spirit to the Father. So
> then you are no longer strangers and aliens, but you are
> citizens with the saints and also members of the
> household of God… (Ephesians 2:14-19).

A New Humanity

If there ever was a person most qualified to speak about the
destruction of that dividing wall, it's the Apostle Paul. Paul had
made an extraordinary, unlikely journey in his own life, and he
had come to change his mind on so many important matters.
Paul had lived his entire life behind the wall of religious
exclusivism. He had been convinced that the covenant that
God had made with the Jews was not a covenant that included
all people. God, he believed, was a Jew, just like Paul, just like

Paul's father, and Paul's grandfather—all the way back to his ancestors in the tribe of Benjamin, where the covenant began. Paul had been so convinced of God's exclusive love for Jews that he hounded and persecuted the early followers of Jesus, who boldly claimed that God's love was for the Gentiles as well as for the Jews. To Paul, this new truth was blasphemy.

The Book of Acts tells us that Paul was on his way to Damascus to hunt down more Christians and to have them arrested when he was knocked off his horse and blinded. For three days he was cared for by a kind man named Ananias, a Christian, who healed Paul, and later baptized him. In that moment, according to the story, something like scales fell from Paul's eyes, like stones from a wall suddenly breaking loose and tumbling down, and Paul came to see a new reality beyond the ancient walls that he had come to accept for so long.

For Paul, that event marked the gradual journey from narrow exclusivism to an open, generous theology of the cross. Over time, Paul came to see that the image of the out-stretched hands of Christ on the cross was a symbol of God's far-reaching, boundless embrace of all of humanity. He came to believe that God sent Jesus not just to save a few fortunate Jews who happened to have won the DNA lottery, but to heal and reconcile the whole creation to God.

By the end of his life, Paul was saying that, in Christ, the dividing wall has been broken down, so that we are no longer strangers and aliens to one another, but neighbors—even members of the same family. Paul believed this so deeply that, as he wrote these words, he was more than willing to give his very life for them. After having ventured beyond the walls of his former life, he had encountered a whole world of Gentiles on the other side of that wall. These Gentiles, upon hearing the message of Christ's boundless love, kept asking Paul if they, too, could become members of this new humanity.

They came in droves to Paul and said:

- "I'm not a Jew, but can I be included?"

- "I don't know anything about your Bible, or about all the purity laws and rituals and requirements of your tradition, but can I be included?"

- "I am a Republican, I am a Palestinian, I am a Mexican, I am a leper, I am a lesbian, I am a convict with a long rap sheet, I am just a child, but can I be included?"

When you read the letters of Paul, it's clear that none of this came easy for him. Paul was as reluctant as you and I when it comes to figuring out who really should be included.

It is never easy to remove even a single stone from the wall you have been living behind, because every time you take one of those stones off the wall, you see another face on the other side of it.

And this is what it says: "What about me?"

Paul was conflicted more times than not. The wall didn't come down all at once for him. He argued and resisted his way through it, one hard stone after another, until the dividing wall of stones finally became one big, towering pile. By the time Paul was done tearing down that wall, the heaping pile of stones that remained became something like an altar to God, a monument to the new humanity we share in Christ. It became a symbol of the end of all the violence, wars, bigotry and misunderstanding and suspicion and fear that makes us strangers to one another.

What that monument says is this: "By the life and death and resurrection of Jesus, we belong to God, every one of us. And because we belong to God, we belong to each other."

If Not You, Then Who?

Presbyterian pastor and author Michael Lindval tells about a friend, Fuad Bahnan, an Arab Christian pastor living in Beirut after the last Arab-Israeli war. In 1983, Israeli armies drove into Lebanon, and members of the church began to buy all the canned food they could in order to survive a rumored Israeli siege. West Beirut had been totally cut-off. And so the leaders of the church met to decide how to distribute the food they had purchased. Two proposals were put on the table. The first was to distribute food to the church members, then other Christians, and finally—if any food was left—to Muslim neighbors.

The other proposal was different. Food would first be given to Muslim neighbors, then to other Christians, and finally—if there was any left over—to church members.

The meeting lasted six hours.

It ended when an older, quiet, much respected Elder, a woman, stood up and said, "If we do not demonstrate the love of Christ in this place, who will?" And so the second motion passed.[13]

You Can Do It, We Can Help

You can do this. You need to get out more, and the first step is identifying the walls that keep you in, that keep others out. Remember, so many of these walls are invisible. They've been passed down from generation to generation. You've lived with them for so long they've become a part of the background. Chances are you don't even know they are there. In order to find them, you'll need to get moving—like Jesus, like the Apostle Paul. Soon enough, you'll bump into those walls. Whether you choose to remain behind them, scale them, or tear them down is up to you.

Last year, over the Martin Luther King, Jr. holiday weekend, members of my congregation left the suburbs and made a four-day pilgrimage into downtown Los Angeles. A work project had been identified ahead of time, something that would require the use of our hands, physical labor, a power tool or two. The "work project" was the lure we used to recruit team members, but the ultimate aim of the trip was to encounter people, enter neighborhoods, experience cultures, and engage traditions that were altogether foreign to us.

We spent an afternoon at Homeboy Industries and got to know some of the homies and home girls, many of whom were heavily tattooed and most of whom were former felons. We visited places like Watts Towers, the L.A. River, and the infamous intersection of Florence and Normandy, where the 1992 L.A. Uprising erupted with the beating of Reginald Denny. We ate together—in Chinatown, in Koreatown, at Mama's Hot Tamales, or at Roscoe's Chicken and Waffles—surrounded by people of diverse cultures and ethnicities and social classes. We walked the crowded sidewalks of Skid Row, visited the missions, talked with the residents. On Sunday morning, we worshipped with an African-American congregation, in traditions and forms of worship unfamiliar to us. In the evenings, we shared with one another about what we had experienced.

Over those four days, we bumped into the walls of race, social class, culture, and traditions. We discovered, like Jesus, like Paul, that these walls are highly porous, that they crumble easily, and that the strangers on the other side of them are our neighbors and members of the household of God.

The Great Permission

Don't ask the world for permission to cross borders. You will encounter resistance from within and from without. The status quo depends on your blind acceptance of the myth that good fences make good neighbors. Don't wait for the world's approval or permission. Help yourself. Just go.

The late Murray Bowen, a psychiatrist who pioneered Family Systems Theory, suggested that within any relational system, whether it's a family, or a church, or a group of close friends, or even a nation, there is a natural tendency towards homeostasis or balance. If the "system" is to survive in the face of problems or challenges or change, everyone in the system must play their prescribed role. This natural tendency toward balance functions like a thermostat—regulating and limiting the range of possibilities and change within the system. Stability is the goal of every relational system, but it's also the greatest impediment to a healthy sense of self. When one member doesn't play his or her prescribed role, someone else will have to compensate in order to maintain the balance. This co-dependency is unhealthy for everyone, hence the need to keep everyone functioning in their own particular roles. And when someone tries to transcend their roles, even for the sake of the system, the system will almost always resist, even sabotage those efforts, in order to maintain the original balance.

This is why Galileo Galilei, convinced that the earth revolved around the sun, was convicted of heresy before the Grand Inquisition and spent the remainder of his life under house arrest.

It's why Giordano Bruno, convinced of "a plurality of worlds"—that is, an infinite number of galaxies—was dragged out to the market square and burned at the stake by well-meaning religious people.

It's why Jesus, when he came home for the first time after launching his public ministry, was rejected by the people of his hometown. They said to Jesus, "Who do you think you are? The Chosen One, the Messiah? Are you kidding me?" And in that moment, Jesus had to make the choice: would he be Jesus of Nazareth or Jesus the Christ?[14]

All great truths begin as blasphemies, and we can all think of a few great blasphemers upon whose shoulders we stand today:

Galileo and Bruno, Martin Luther and John Calvin, Susan B. Anthony and Elizabeth Cady Stanton, Dr. King and Nelson Mandela, Aung Sang Suk Kyi and Dorothy Day. Each one of them could see truths that the rest of the world refused to accept.

Sometimes you have to give yourself permission. If you wait around for the world to open up doors for you, chances are you'll be forever stuck at the starting line. There is a time and a place for knocking on doors, seizing opportunities, creating new realities, tearing down walls.

For Christians, permission to do so is grounded in the Great Commission: "Go, therefore, into all the world," commanded Jesus. "Preach the Good News. Practice the Good News. Be the Good News."[15] It's a reminder that you don't need to ask the world for its permission to make a difference. Over and over again, Jesus said, "Go and do."

On most days, that's all the permission you need.

Hospitality Apps

Adventures in the Neighborhood

1. Take a ride on a city bus. On a city bus, you will encounter people of extraordinary diversity: age, race, nationality, social class, language, etc. Drop a token, find a seat next to a complete stranger, and strike up a conversation.

2. Join or create a prison or jail ministry in your local church. Many churches and Christian organizations (such as *Kairos Prison Ministry* or *Get on the Bus*) bring the message of God's boundless love to the incarcerated and their families through faith-sharing, listening, worship and correspondence.

3. Visit your local Islamic Center, Masjid, or mosque. Arrange for a tour, interview the Imam, learn about the values and mission of your Muslim neighbors.

4. Volunteer at a local soup kitchen. In addition to serving a meal, be sure to take the time to sit with the guests and share in conversation.

5. Attend a local chapter meeting of the Democratic or Republican Party. Most local chapters are very hospitable to guests of both political parties. Go in a spirit of openness and gentleness, eager to listen and learn.

6. Learn about the international refugees in your area. The International Rescue Committee[16] operates in nearly every major US city, providing resources and advocacy to the displaced and most vulnerable persons among us, while educating the public about their plight. Visit, volunteer, get involved.

7. Visit a worship service in which you will be a minority. Stay after the service and get to know the members of the congregation.

"I will open my mouth to speak in parables; I will proclaim what has been hidden from the foundation of the world."

—Matthew 13:35

3

Spin a Yarn

YOU NEED TO GET OUT MORE and listen deeply to the lives of those who share the sidewalk with you. We live in a culture that does not foster deep conversation between people. More and more, we are becoming a generation dependent upon sound bites, small talk, bumper-sticker declarations, tweets and text messages under 140 characters. We talk at one another, but we don't know how to speak *with* one another. Watch the evening news, attend a town hall meeting, listen to a political debate or to some of the most popular preachers on television, and you will see how much of our public discourse conveys the ideas and principles and beliefs we stand *for*, and those which we stand *against*. But those who desire to live the hospitable life will, like Jesus, find creative ways to talk about whom they stand *with*. By sharing our stories and listening deeply to the stories of others, we come to see our common humanity. Moreover, we come to see more honestly how our own stories belong to the larger narrative of God's grace, which binds us to one another in the household of God.

If you've ever listened to *Morning Edition* on National Public Radio, you've likely heard of the weekly series called *StoryCorps*. *StoryCorps* is an independent nonprofit whose mission is to provide Americans of all backgrounds and beliefs with the opportunity to record, share, and preserve the stories of their lives. Since 2003, *StoryCorps* has collected and archived more than 40,000 interviews from nearly 80,000 participants. The purpose of the project is to remind one another of our shared humanity, strengthen the connections between people, teach the value of listening, and weave into the fabric of our culture the understanding that every life matters. At the same time, an invaluable archive of American voices and wisdom is created for future generations.

More often than not, when I listen to a story on *StoryCorps*, I hear hints of my own story. The storyteller could not be more different from me—a Sikh from San Francisco, a first-responder at the World Trade Center on September 11, a sixty year old man with spina bifida—and yet their hopes and their hurts are, in many ways, not unlike my own. They are courageous, grateful, regretful, conflicted, at peace, full of pride, full of doubt. They laugh, they cry, they sometimes do not know what they feel, or what they believe, or what their experiences really mean to them, or to others.

But they know their story. And in telling their story, they invite me into some of the most intimate, vulnerable, pregnant moments of their lives. In listening to their story, I begin to hear how God's Holy Spirit is working in and through them, and I begin to see them with the kind of grace and tenderness with which God sees them.

This practice of sharing our stories with one another is an essential habit of hospitable living. It takes us out of our own limited worlds, and reveals to us a broader understanding of our connectedness to others, our purpose, and God's reign.

It is said that Alex Haley, the late author of *Roots*, learned the whole saga—the story that would later become a Pulitzer-Prize winning book—while sitting on his grandparent's front porch. As a child growing up in Henning, Tennessee in the 1920s, Haley sat spellbound on the front porch of his grandparents' home listening to his maternal grandmother, Cynthia Palmer, tell stories of his African ancestors who had come to America as slaves. They included Kunta Kinte, a young man captured near his West African village and transported on a slave ship to America in the 18th century. These stories, told from a front porch, later inspired Haley to research his ancestry and write the novel that changed the way an entire generation would come to understand the history of our nation, the plight of a people, and the evils of slavery.

It all began with a story told on a front porch.

A Better Story

The prophet Joel reminds us of the importance of telling stories and keeping alive the flame that is our heritage: "Tell your children about it in years to come, and let your children tell their children. Pass the story down from generation to generation" (Joel 1:3). When was the last time you told a story about your late father, or your mother's mother, or, as Haley called Kunta Kinte, the "furthest-back person" in your life? When was the last time you asked a friend or a neighbor about his or her life story? Have you ever told someone your own life story?

When you know your own story—both the memorable and even the forgettable parts—you know yourself more fully. When you share that story with others, as Haley did his own, others come to know you more fully, and perhaps they even come to know more of themselves, or the self they would like to be.

My son Casey was given an assignment for his high school history class: to interview a World War II veteran about his experiences in war. I arranged for Casey to meet with an old friend of mine—someone whose life and life story I have come to greatly admire over the years. After the interview, Casey said, "I just talked with one of the most amazing people I have ever met. Just hearing his story makes me want to be a better person."

When you hear a good story, it makes you want to live a better story. We need to get out more and swap stories.

What's Your Story?

Storytelling is universal. In every culture humans have learned to cast their personal identity in some sort of narrative form. Whether you realize it or not, you perceive your own life in grand story form. Over the many years you have been given to live to this point, you have sought to make meaning of the events and experiences and encounters in your life—the hardships and the victories, the conflicts and the conquests, the antagonists and the champions, the serendipities and the banalities.

These have shaped who you are today, including your self-understanding, your worldview, your assumptions about others, your relationships with friends and strangers, and even your understanding of God's presence and agency in your life. These events and experiences will have some degree of influence on the choices you will make and the person you will be tomorrow because, taken together, they help to form a particular pattern by which you have come to perceive—and live—your life.

Your life has a storyline. Your life is a story. It contains all the essential elements of a good story:

- It's about a Character.
- It's about a Character that wants something.
- It's about a Character has gone through conflict to get what he or she wants.
- It's about a Character that has experienced transformation as a result of conflict.[17]

You are the protagonist in your life story. And your life story, like every good story, has a plot, a theme, and a narrative arc.

The *plot* of your life story is not simply what has happened to you, but the pattern of how you, in the face of conflict or obstacles, have acted to resolve such conflicts or overcome such obstacles. You may be unsatisfied with that resolution. You may have run away from conflicts or avoided obstacles. You may have resolved them heroically, or quietly, or inconclusively. Nevertheless, when you add them up, you begin to see a pattern. This is your plot.

The *theme* of your life story is the meaning you have drawn from the plot as it has played out so far. Your responses to the conflict in your life, and the changes that it has produced in you (good or bad), contribute to the theme of your life story. Those who successfully overcome conflict repeatedly might say, "Nothing is impossible with God," or "When the tough get going," or "I'm a survivor." These are predominant life themes in our culture.

Likewise, those who do not regularly overcome their conflict might say, "Because [*fill in the blank*] has happened to me, I will never be the same again." Or "If I only had more [*money, education, time, power, influence, etc.*], my life would be different." Or, as Timone says in *The Lion King*, "When the world turns it's back on you, you turn your back on the world." These too are predominant life themes in our culture.

The *narrative arc* of your life story is the broader pattern or trajectory that your life has taken to this point. The Greeks, who mastered the art of storytelling through drama and theater, taught us to think of a story as having three "acts" or stages—a beginning, a middle, and an end. A good story moves from Exposition (who the character is, where the character lives, what the character desires), to Rising Action (the conflicts and obstacles to achieving that desire, such as The Wicked Witch, or Lord Voldemort, or Darth Vader), to Resolution (getting Dorothy and Toto back home, or preventing Voldemort from getting the stone, or saving the Empire).

Your life story, however, is different. It's not finished. Your character is constantly evolving. There are stories within your story. There have been many conflicts and obstacles. You overcame some of them. Others got the best of you. Still others are yet unresolved. Your narrative arc probably looks more like a roller coaster, with many ups and downs, twists and loops. It's still unfolding.

But remember, too, that the narrative arc of your life story actually began long before you were born. Your story has been shaped, in some measure, by your ancestors—those "furthest-back people" in your family. You have inherited traditions, assumptions, biases, family secrets, legacies, expectations. Some of these have made you who you are; perhaps some of them have kept you from becoming who you are.

If you look back over the course of your life—even into the distant past of your family tree—and begin to chart the smaller stories that have made you who you are today, you'll start to see a pattern emerge. When you map out the highs and the lows along a timeline that represents your life, you may begin to see a plot, notice patterns, and even identify a unifying theme.

Before you read any further, put down this book, reach for a sheet of paper and a pen, draw a timeline, and chart the conflicts and obstacles, the victories and disappointments, the people and places of your past. These might include: the day you were born, the day your grandfather died, the marathon you ran, the bankruptcy, the baby, the break-up, the new job. They might also include saints and sinners on your family tree—even those you may never have known, but whose legacy has shaped who you are.

When you are finished, ask yourself:

- If someone were to read the story of my life, how would they describe the character that is me?
- What is it that this character wants?
- What have been the obstacles, the conflicts that have stood in the way?

- How have these many obstacles and conflicts changed the character, in both good ways and bad?

- Finally, considering what has been resolved and what has yet to be resolved, what are some of the emerging themes of this story?

What it Feels Like

A couple of years ago I came across a little book by the curious title, *What it Feels Like*. Published by *Esquire*, the book offers more than fifty true, first-person accounts of those who have endured some of life's most exhilarating, harrowing, or bizarre experiences. If you've ever wondered what it feels like to go over Niagara Falls in a barrel, or to be attacked by a grizzly bear, or to jump from a plane only to have your parachute fail, or to suffer from narcolepsy or the Ebola Virus or from obsessive-compulsive disorder and the chronic impulse to wash your hair sixty times a day until it hurts—this book will inform you. It may even inspire you, as with Buzz Aldrin's account of walking on the moon, or the story of a sole survivor of an airline crash.[18]

There's something about listening to another person's life, especially their struggle in the face of adversity and their determination to overcome—it has a way of inspiring us, perhaps even healing us. The stories of others have the power, if we listen carefully, to teach us something about our own lives, because in hearing another person's story of the aches and awes of life, we often overhear our *own* stories—the betrayals we've endured, the tragedies we've survived, the moments of exhilaration and wonder, of despair and defeat; the daring spirit within us all that struggles to overcome the odds.

Why was *Tuesday's with Morrie* a top-ten national best seller for over four years? Because it's the kind of story that not only puts a very real human face to the battle against Lou Gehrig's disease; it also gives us an honest glimpse of our own universal suffering and fear of death, and the wisdom and grace that can be plumbed from the depths of even the worst of human hardship and loss.

This is the real value of knowing your story, and listening deeply to the stories of others. As C.S. Lewis said, "We read to know that we are not alone." The same is true when we swap stories. A moment of genuine hospitality—living in God's generous welcome—occurs whenever real stories are shared because we discover, as Frederick Buechner suggests, that "My story is important not because it is mine, God knows, but because if I tell it anything like right, the chances are you will recognize that in many ways it is also yours."[19]

A Good Story About a Man Named Joseph

If you're not sure you have a good enough story to tell, read your Bible and take heart: the Bible is full of characters—some of them quite sketchy people—who want something and who must overcome conflict to get it. Curiously, much of that conflict—especially early in the Bible—is family conflict. The Book of Genesis begins with people doing very terrible things to each other, most of which have profound and lasting consequences for their lives. Adam and Eve break the only rule God puts before them and are immediately kicked out of paradise because of it; one of their sons, Cain, ends up offing his brother, Abel, in a fit of jealousy—the first act of physical violence in the new world, by the way, and it takes place between brothers. It gets worse as you read on: Jacob steals the birthright from Esau and Esau spends the better part of his life hunting down his brother in anger and vengeance; Judah, in an embarrassing lapse of judgment, sleeps with his own daughter-in-law, Tamar, which produced not just one "oops" baby, but two.

Betrayal, treachery, greed, lust, revenge, and murder—it's better drama than *The Sopranos*. Just open your Bible to Genesis and it's all right there. Real characters. Real conflict.

And it gets even better.

In Genesis 45, the story of Joseph seems to top them all. There is mystery, scheming, foreign intrigue, passion and revenge—all in one single family, like a good Shakespearean tragedy.

Joseph is Jacob's boy. Jacob is the son of Isaac, who is the son of Abraham, who is the father of the Hebrew people. Joseph is one of eleven sons in Jacob's family, and Joseph believes he is the best of them all. He gets out of bed every morning and looks at himself in the mirror and announces that he is the next big thing. At least that's what his dreams tell him, and Joseph has so many dreams that he cannot keep them to himself. His dreams tell him that one day his brothers will fall down at his feet and worship him, and when Joseph tells his brothers about those dreams, his brothers are more than just a little annoyed. It's those dreams, along with the fact that he is very good looking and the apple of his father's eye, that lead the brothers to do the one thing that would change the world forever, only they have no idea at the time how it would all turn out.

One day down in Dothan the brothers decide they have had enough of Joseph and the special robe his father had given to him. They first conspire to kill him, but one of the brothers, Rueben, suggested that throwing him into a deep pit would do the trick just as well, so that's what they do. Just when they are about to leave him for dead, a traveling salesman from Gilead drops by and offers to buy Joseph for twenty pieces of silver. The only thing better than a dead Joseph was a ransom for Joseph, so they cut the deal, and figure that Mr. Big Shot Joseph is gone for good.

Betrayed by his brothers, sold into slavery in Egypt, unjustly imprisoned for two years—you could say Joseph has a serious score to settle with his brothers if ever given the chance. But something happens to Joseph that marks a dramatic change in the course of events. Joseph, the master of dreams, begins interpreting the dreams of a few prisoners in jail; before long, Pharaoh is told of Joseph's uncanny gift, and sends for Joseph, that he might interpret a few of Pharaoh's troubling dreams.

Joseph is so good at interpreting Pharaoh's dreams that Pharaoh promotes Joseph to be head of Egypt's Department of Agriculture. Just like that, Joseph is Pharaoh's second-in-command. Over the next seven years Joseph sees to it that Egypt stores up enough food to survive the coming famine, which Pharaoh's dreams had predicted according to Joseph's interpretations.

When the famine finally arrives, it is felt all the way over in the land of Canaan, where Jacob and his ten sons are beginning to feel the pinch of a no-carb, no-calorie, New South Canaan diet. And when word gets out that Egypt has food, the ten brothers are sent to Egypt to buy some, which is when the story comes full circle.

Time out: years ago you were sold by your family for 20 pieces of silver. You spent years in prison, enduring unimaginable abuse, losing everything that mattered to you, only to overcome it all and rise up to become a powerful world leader. Now, years later, that same family arrives on your doorstep, pleading for your hospitality. It's been so long that they do not even recognize you.

What are you thinking, Joseph? An eye for an eye, a life for a life? Someone has to pay for the tragedy that has become your life. You are, after all, the victim.

Only Joseph doesn't see it that way; he doesn't see himself that way. When he looks at his life he does not see a series of painful tragedies from which he would never recover. What he sees instead is something like a series of seemingly random dots, spread out across the dark canvas of his dreams like stars in the black sky; to an ordinary person, those dots of his painful experiences would look senseless, meaningless, random. Call it fate, or bad luck, one meaningless tragedy after another.

But when Joseph looks at that same canvas, he sees a pattern emerging. Looking back over the course of his life, he begins to connect the dots, from the dark, deep pit in Dothan, to the hard labor in Egypt, to two years in Pharaoh's bleak prison cell, to this very moment standing before his brothers, more free now than they had ever been, more powerful now than they would ever be.

What he sees when he connects all those dots is the most complete image of himself that he has ever before had; he sees that, because of his unique journey, his very life has been fashioned now into an instrument of God, ordained for this very crucial moment in the history of God's chosen people. Joseph can see that God had preserved him so that he could save his brothers from famine and ensure that the people of God would survive.

"I am Joseph," he says to them. "Come closer to me. I am your brother, whom you sold off for twenty pieces of silver."

To his brothers, this sounds like very bad news.

But listen to what Joseph says next:

> And now, do not be distressed and do not be angry with yourselves for selling me here, because it was to save lives that God sent me ahead of you. For two years now there has been famine in the land, and for the next five years there will be no plowing and reaping. But God sent me ahead of you to preserve for you a remnant on earth and to save your lives by a great deliverance. So then, it was not you who sent me here, but God (Genesis 45:5-8).

Then he drew them near him, and he wept upon their necks, and kissed them.

Joseph's story is a story about how people of faith, in the face of real hardship and adversity, have a choice in how their story will unfold, and what their story will mean. Joseph discovered that he was not only the character in his story, but the editor.

Connect the Dots

You have a story. You need to get out more and tell it, because it has the power to heal people. Like Joseph's story, it may even have the power to save people. God has given you the freedom to connect the dots in your life story—the ache and the awe of it, the victories and the defeats, the terrible things you have endured and the hard things you have yet to understand. God has given you the freedom to look at all of it, to see it for what it really is. And then God holds his breath and waits to see what you will make of it.

Will you connect the dots, even the painful dots that you once thought had left a part of your life too bent and broken to be useful? Will you connect those dots to discover a deeper revelation of a life story that looks like something God can use for a higher, more holy purpose?

God is not the sole author of your life story. You are not the sole author of your story. Both you and God are the editors of your life story, working together to create a better story.

Know your story. Learn to share it. Get out and tell it graciously, with humility. And remember: leave off the final period at the end of it. Your story is not finished.

Enough About Me

"We live in a world where bad stories are told," writes Donald Miller,

stories that teach us life doesn't mean anything and that
humanity has no great purpose. It's a good calling,
then, to speak a better story... How grateful we are to
hear these stories, and how happy it makes us to repeat
them.[20]

We need to become better storytellers. We also need to
become better at listening to the stories of others. We need to
learn how to listen to one another more deeply.

Most of us are quite adept at selective listening. When
someone speaks, we often hear only what we want to hear, or
at least what we think is most important to hear, mostly for our
own sake. *How does this affect me? What are the essential details that
I need to know?*

Sometimes we succumb to partial listening. We have the
best intentions of hearing what the other is saying, but we
become distracted by stray thoughts (*"Did I pay the mortgage this
month?"*), or by something the other person has said (*"What did
he mean by that?" "I can't believe she just said that..."*).

But deep listening is rare. When you listen deeply, you're
hearing not only the whole story, but the whole person behind
the story. You listen between the lines of what is shared, giving
attention to emotions, needs, goals and values, biases and
beliefs, even body language—all without personal judgment.

Carl Rogers, the late American psychologist, pioneered the
habit of "active listening," a practice of repeating back or
paraphrasing what you think you are hearing and gently seeking
clarification when the meaning is not clear. It requires the
listener to suspend judgment, to disentangle one's own
experiences, assumptions, and anxieties from what is being
shared. The ultimate goal of deep, active listening is not
agreement, but understanding.

Tell Me Something I Don't Know

Find someone you trust, and who trusts you—a neighbor, a friend, a co-worker, a member at your church. Take them out for coffee, or invite them into your home. Go for a long walk with them. Sit around a campfire with them. Do whatever seems natural. This doesn't need to feel like a *Taster's Choice* kind of moment. Just be yourself. And when the Spirit leads you, just ask them:

- Will you tell me about an experience you have had that changed the direction of your life?

- Will you share with me a story about someone who has influenced you?

- Will you tell me why you chose your current vocation?

- Will you share with me how you have experienced the grace of God in your life?

You can probably think of some questions on your own. Ask them.

You may get resistance. Accept this.

You may get a longer story than anticipated. Honor this.

You may get nothing at all. Respect this.

But you may hear a very good story. You may hear a story that you recognize as your own. You may hear a story that makes you want to live a better story. You may even hear a story that sounds something like a gospel story.

A Bad Story Made Good

Sitting at a table in a Starbucks several years ago, I peered over the screen of my laptop and watched a tattooed man remove his black leather jacket and pull up a chair at the table next to me. Scanning the room somewhat furtively, he appeared to be waiting for someone to arrive. And about five minutes later, she walked in.

They shook hands, introduced themselves to each other and ordered their coffees before sitting down. Their conversation was clearly audible. They had apparently made a connection through an online dating service of some kind.

"You look different than your on-line profile," she said.

He offered a subtle laugh. "Do you want to leave already?" he asked her.

"Oh no," she said. "It's just that it's happened before. I meet someone online, but they're someone different in person."

They were already off to a rocky start. They both fumbled awkwardly with their cups for a few moments, as if they'd rather be anywhere else but there.

"So...," she said, "tell me about yourself. What's your story?"

He took a long pause, a heavy breath, and said, "It's pretty straightforward. Let's see: I've been shot twice, stabbed once, and I was just released from prison."

She laughed. "No, really," she said.

I peeked over my computer screen. He paused again, this time longer.

"Really," he said. "No kidding. I did some things, you know... I paid a heavy price, but I found God...or God found me. I'm trying to start over."

She was speechless, her face suddenly ashen. Her jaw seemed to hang loosely from her face. She glanced briefly at the door, then forced a half-hearted smile.

He said, "Look, I'll totally understand if you want to leave right now. It's what I have to deal with now. I can't change the past. Do you want to leave? You can leave. Do you want to leave?"

She took a long stare into her coffee cup, then glanced at her watch. When she looked back at him, it seemed like she was all at once looking at some deeper place inside of him, or to some place inside of him that offered a reflection of a place inside of her.

"Do you want to leave," he asked her again? "I'll understand. You can leave."

She took a deep breath, and exhaled.

"Well," she said, "we really just sat down. I'm in no real hurry."

She leaned back in her chair, took a sip from her no-whip, non-fat, half-caf grande vanilla latte, and set the cup back on the table.

"So," she said. "Tell me—who are you now?"

You need to get out more and swap good stories. Jesus spent his entire ministry getting out, moving from town to town, telling good stories—about homesick prodigals and merciful fathers, about forsaken sojourners and good Samaritans, about determined shepherds searching all night for one lost sheep, about persistent women and rich fools and unforgiving servants and pearls of great price. The stories Jesus told had the power to save people, and they still do.

Know your story. Learn to share it. Tell it humbly.

Listen to the stories of others—deeply, generously.

And remember: whether you are telling a story or listening to one, leave off the final period at the end of it, because the story being told is not yet finished.

Hospitality Apps

Adventures in the Neighborhood

1. Participate in the National Day of Listening[21], a new national holiday started by *StoryCorps* in 2008. On the day after Thanksgiving, *StoryCorps* asks all Americans to take an hour to record an interview with a loved one, using recording equipment that is readily available in most homes, such as computers, iPhones, and tape recorders, along with *StoryCorps'* free Do-It-Yourself Instruction Guide.

2. Journal or blog about your experiences, paying close attention not simply to what has happened to you, but the meaning you have drawn from such experiences.

3. Sit down with the "furthest back person" in your family, or in your church, or in your neighborhood, and ask them to tell you a story about their childhood, or their family, or their first love, or their first loss or disappointment.

4. Make a list of as many of your favorite Bible stories as you can remember. What makes these stories memorable to you? What characters do you seem most apt to identify with? What themes and plots seem to resonate with those of your own?

5. Establish a pen pal relationship with a person in prison. Share your story. Inquire about their story.[22]

"Go therefore into the main streets, and invite everyone you
find to the wedding banquet."

—Matthew 22:9

4

Set the Table

I WAS TALKING TO A FRIEND OF MINE who spends a lot of time on the road, traveling across the country as a consultant. He spends more than two-thirds of his life on the road, bouncing from city to city. We were talking about the toll that traveling can take on a person—the hotels, the airports, the time zones. Over time, it all adds up. But he said the hardest part about being on the road so much is eating alone. "Sitting at a table by yourself, two or three times a day—you just never get used to eating alone."

The first meal recorded in Scripture—a piece of fruit from the forbidden tree—was a meal eaten alone (Genesis 3). The last meal recorded in Scripture—the feast of the Heavenly Kingdom—is a generous banquet shared in community (Revelation 7). Our spiritual journey is a movement from brokenness and aloneness to wholeness and community, and food plays a central role in that redemptive passage.

Scattered across the pages of the gospels—especially Luke's Gospel—are images of the dinner table. For Jesus, the dinner table was not merely the place at which one eats, but where people gather with others to learn, study, share, confess, forgive, celebrate, encourage and pray. For Jesus, the dinner table is the hub of hospitality in the Kingdom of God.

In Luke's Gospel, if you want to find Jesus, look for the nearest dinner table. You'll find him at the home of Zacchaeus, the dreaded tax collector whom everyone loathes—the local Tony Soprano—who scampered up the sycamore tree to spy Jesus as he passed by. When Jesus saw him, he said, "Zacchaeus, let's go have dinner at your house" (Luke 19).

On another occasion, Jesus stops by the home of Mary and Martha and, while sitting around the dinner table, teaches them about the Kingdom of God (Luke 10). Invited to dinner by Simon the Pharisee, Jesus sits at the table with the other guests and, before the night is over, teaches about hospitality and the forgiveness of sins (Luke 7). While vacationing with his disciples in Bethsaida, Jesus multiplies five loaves of bread and two fish into a feast for 5,000 people (Luke 9).

One evening, after Jesus had taught his best friends everything they would need to know upon his death, he sets the table for twelve. Even Judas, his betrayer, is welcomed at this table. With bread and wine, he tells each of them how much he loves them. Holding a loaf of bread in his hands, he says, "This is my body, given for you" (Luke 22).

After his death, the risen Jesus meets the crestfallen Cleopas and his friend on the lonely road to Emmaus. Jesus appears to them as a mere stranger, but when they invite him to dinner that evening, their hope is restored. "When he was at the table with them, he took bread, blessed and broke it, and gave it to them. Then their eyes were opened, and they recognized him" (Luke 24:30-31).

Wherever there's a table, wherever food is shared, you'll find Jesus. As Leonard Sweet suggests, the Jesus movement was a culinary revolution that invited people to "taste and see" the goodness of God:

> Jesus spoke the language of food. He used food to teach, heal, build community, transform village life, and break down walls of alienation and oppression... To eat all kinds of food, clean and unclean, was the daily expression of the theological revolution Jesus effected, whereby everybody became brothers and sisters in the new household of faith, even those who were previously declared "unclean:" the disabled, Samaritans,

women, publicans, half-breeds, minors, and sinners...
In the Scriptures, Jesus is frequently eating "good food
with bad people.[23]

There is no greater symbol of our common bond in the
household of God than the dinner table. There is no more
tangible sign of our genuine love and acceptance of one
another than our willingness—our eagerness—to share our
bread with one another. At the table, strangers and
acquaintances become friends. At the table, there is
opportunity for true companionship—a word that comes from
the Latin, *companis*, which means, literally, "with bread." A
companion is someone with whom you share bread.

Jesus loved to eat. Usually not alone. He ate with friends.
He ate with strangers. He ate with sinners. By the time he
finally pushed himself away from the table, they had become
his companions.

Table for Two

I landed my first steady job when I was fifteen years old. My
boss was an eighty-three year old widow who, for $4 an hour,
paid me to do some light chores at her modest mobile home.
Every Saturday at 8:00am, she would give me a list of things to
do—wash the windows, sweep the patio, pull the weeds out
front. At around 10:30am, she would call me into her single
wide trailer for a break, whereupon we would sit at her small
dining table and, over a plate of cookies and a glass of milk, we
would talk.

At noon, she would call me in again: a plate of potato chips,
a ham and cheese sandwich, cut into four crust-less squares, a
few pecan sandies, and a glass of soda that had long since lost
its fizz. There, at the table, we ate and talked.

At 2:30, more cookies, milk, conversation.

I was fifteen years old and didn't fully understand at the time the exact nature of my work: seven hours of chores and an hour and a half of conversation, once a week for three years. She would have me pull weeds that were no longer there, wash windows that still sparkled from the week before, and vacuum her spotless floor. It took me a few visits before it finally clicked for me: six days a week she ate alone, but one day a week she had someone at her table.

Over the years, around that table, she shared with me the story of her life. I learned about her late husband's inventions, her long trip west in the days of the Dust Bowl, about the day she learned how to drive and the day she was told that she could no longer drive. We shuffled through old black and white photographs of a bygone world, and read the poetry of Wordsworth and Dickinson, and talked about my family, my girlfriends, my hopes and dreams. We did all of this while eating little crust-less squares of ham and cheese sandwiches and drinking orange soda around a small dining table.

Her name was Rose Pringle, and she taught me that there is nothing more spiritual, nothing more mutually redemptive, than to share your food at the table.

The Guest List

A woman was being interviewed by a reporter from a local newspaper. This particular woman had just celebrated her 104th birthday, and so the reporter asked her, "Considering everything you've experienced over the course of your long life, what's the best thing about being 104?" The woman gave serious thought to the question, and then replied: "No peer pressure."

In every one of us, there is an inherent, almost incessant longing to "find our place" in the social structures of this world—to fit in. Whether we are sitting at the elementary school lunch table on our first day of school, or trying out for the high school basketball team, or pledging for the college fraternity or sorority, or attending a dinner party in our new neighborhood, every one of us knows at least a little of what it's like to seek, to struggle, and sometimes even fail to "find our place"—to belong, to fit in, to be accepted, to be granted a place to sit at the so-called "cool kids' table."

And so, at a very early age, we learn the social tactics of sizing people up, of discerning who can help us get what we want and who's to be avoided altogether; of learning the unwritten rules and unspoken assumptions of the group we aspire to be a part of; of separating in our minds those who belong and those who do not; of working our way in and up the ladder, carefully, subtlety, even strategically.

In just about every human circle of relationships—at school, at work, in our neighborhoods, even in our families—there are those who possess social power and those who wish they had it.

It's what C.S. Lewis once called the phenomenon of the "Inner Ring." Lewis said that each of us has a life-long desire—from infancy to old age—to be inside what he called the *local ring*. The local ring is an exclusive social circle where power and importance and superiority are bestowed upon the select few who are fortunate enough to be included. But Lewis also said that deep in the psyche of every one of us is the life-long fear of being left outside of the Ring, of not belonging to whatever social circle that we most desperately want for ourselves. This drive to be included, and the accompanying fear of being excluded, is what Lewis called the lust for the esoteric: the desperate longing to be inside. He said that, while an inner-ring is not necessarily a bad thing, whenever we become an "inner-ringer," we open ourselves up to becoming *scoundrels*, as he called it. Lewis says it might happen like this:

> Over a drink or a cup of coffee, disguised as a triviality and sandwiched between two jokes, from the lips of a man or woman whom you have recently been getting to

know rather better and whom you hope to know better still—just at the moment when you are most anxious not to appear crude or naïve—the hint will come. It will be the hint of something which is not quite in accordance with the technical rules of fair play: something, says your new friend, which "we"—and at the word "we" you try not to blush for mere pleasure—something, says your friend, "which we always do." And you will be drawn in... simply because at that moment, when the cup was so near your lips, you cannot bear to be thrust back again into the cold outer world. It would be so terrible to see the other man's face—that genial, confidential, sophisticated face—turn suddenly cold and contemptuous, to know that you had been tried for the Inner Ring and rejected. And then, if you *are* drawn in, next week it will be something a little further from the rules, and next year something further still, but all in the jolliest, friendliest spirit. It may end in a crash: it may end in millions. But you will be a scoundrel...

Of all the passions, says Lewis, "the passion for the Inner Ring is most skillful in making a man who is not yet a very bad man do very bad things."[24]

This drive to be included, and the accompanying fear of being rejected, can become a life-long concern for some of us—even for those who, believing in their own goodness, would never intend to do "very bad things."

In Luke 14, Jesus attends a dinner party with some very religious people. They are among the religious elite, men who have made their way into *the inner ring*. They are the same good, religious people who, in the end, will build a case against Jesus and call for his crucifixion.

They invite Jesus to dinner in order to figure him out and decide where exactly he fits in, if indeed he fits in at all. But they already suspect that he does not, given what they've heard about all the heretical things he's said and done—not the least of which is healing on the Sabbath and keeping company with prostitutes and tax collectors. So they invite Jesus to dinner in order to watch him very closely, but as all the dinner guests arrive for the evening, Jesus stands back and watches them as they jockey for a place at the table.

First-century dining hierarchy is serious business. There are very strict rules: priests at the top of the table, then Levites, then other guests according to rank and status—so that those at the very end, those furthest from the host would be the least important of the guests. Everyone has their proper place. In the first-century world, the dinner table is the fundamental symbol of social order, a portrait of society—how it is to be structured, where people are classified on the social ladder, who matters, who is to be included.

But after carefully watching the guests jockey awkwardly around the table, arguing over who should sit higher than whom, Jesus interrupts them. He makes the bold suggestion that the guests ought to sit down at the lowest place, so that when the host comes, he may say to the guest, "Friend, move up higher." In this way, says Jesus, you'll know where you really stand, and you'll be "honored in the presence of all who sit at the table with you. For all who exalt themselves will be humbled, and those who humble themselves will be exalted" (Luke 14:11). In other words, genuine acceptance into the Inner Ring is a gift offered graciously by the host rather than grasped desperately by the guest.

Dinner with Schmucks

But Jesus is not finished with his dinner table lesson. He suggests that we've gotten our guest lists wrong. We've invited the wrong crowd to the party. Sitting at the table, he tells them a parable:

'When you give a luncheon or a dinner, do not invite your friends or your brothers or your relatives or rich neighbors, in case they may invite you in return, and you would be repaid. But when you give a banquet, invite the poor, the crippled, the lame, and the blind. And you will be blessed, because they cannot repay you' (Luke 14:11).

Don't ask anybody who can pay you back. Instead, invite the poor who won't know how much money you spent on the silverware. Invite the crippled and the lame who won't be jockeying over positions, but will be grateful just to sit down. Invite the blind, who won't be star-struck by candelabras and fine china and crème brulee. Invite the powerless who are accustomed to eating TV dinners at a card table. Invite the desperately hungry who are not accustomed to eating much at all.

Whether you think it's a good idea or a bad one, there's certainly no logic to it. If you aspire to belong to the Inner Ring, it's illogical to offer a gift to someone without the unspoken expectation that it would, in some way, be repaid. This is what keeps us inside the Inner Ring, and determines who gets in: reciprocity. The "Inner Ringer" keeps an imaginary chalk board in his mind, keeping track of how much he's done for so-and-so, who owes him one, and who never seems to get around to returning the favor.

But the Kingdom table hosted by Jesus is defined not by reciprocity, but by generosity. The feast is extravagant. There are no favors to be repaid there. All are invited, all are generously fed, and there is genuine community among the circle of companions who gather around it. It is the table of abundant living, available to all:

Ho, everyone who thirsts, come to the waters;
    and you that have no money, come, buy and eat!

Come, buy wine and milk without money and without
price.

Why do you spend your money for that which is not
bread, and your labor for that which does not
satisfy?

Listen carefully to me, and eat what is good, and delight
yourselves in rich food.

Incline your ear, and come to me; listen, so that you
may live (Isaiah 55:1-3).

The Kingdom table is a foretaste of the feast of heaven. It's
the Communion table, where it doesn't matter where you've
come from or what you've accomplished or how high you've
climbed up the ladder. All that's required is an honest
admission that, after all our striving after so many Inner Rings,
there's still an emptiness, a loneliness that Jesus, in the presence
of his companions, promises to satisfy.

Fred Craddock tells the story of traveling to the University
of Winnipeg to give a lecture. It was mid-October, but when
he got up on Saturday morning to give the lecture, two or three
feet of snow pressed against the door. The lecture was
cancelled, and the airport was closed. He walked to a café at
the little bus depot around the corner, where every stranded
traveler in western Canada had gathered—strangers to each
other, pressing and pushing and loud. He finally found a place
to sit in the café, and a man in a greasy apron came over.
Craddock said, "May I see a menu?" The man said, "What do
you want a menu for? We have soup." Craddock said, "What
kinds of soup do you have?" The man barked, "Soup. You
want some soup?" Craddock replied, "That was what I was
going to order—soup."

He brought the soup, and I put the spoon to it... It
was the color and flavor of a grey mouse; it was so bad
I couldn't eat it, but I sat there and put my hands about

it... The door opened again. The wind was icy. In came this woman clutching her little coat. She found a place. The greasy apron came, "What do you want?" She said, "A glass of water." He brought a glass of water, took out his tablet, and said, "Now what'll you have?" She said, "Just the water." He said, "You have to order, lady." "Well, I just want a glass of water," she said. He said, "Look. I have customers that pay—what do you think this is, a church or something? Now what do you want?" She said, "Just a glass of water and some time to get warm." He said, "If you're not going to order, you've got to leave!" And he got real loud about it. So she got up to leave and, almost as if rehearsed, everybody in that little café stood up and started toward the door...and the man in the greasy apron said, "All right, all right, she can stay." Everybody sat down, and he brought her a bowl of soup.

Craddock asked a man sitting next to him, 'Who is she?' The man said, 'I never saw her before.' The place grew quiet, and Craddock says, "I heard the sipping of that awful soup." He decided to try that awful soup again.

I put my spoon to the soup—you know, it was not bad soup. Everybody was eating this soup. I started eating the soup, and it was pretty good soup. I have no idea what kind of soup it was. I don't know what was in it, but... it reminded me of something. I couldn't remember what it was at the time, but I knew I had tasted it before. And later, it finally came to me. That soup—it tasted a little bit like... bread and wine. Just a little like bread and wine.[25]

Wherever there is food, Jesus is present. Whenever that food is shared with others, the meal becomes a messianic banquet of revolutionary consequences. There is physical and spiritual sustenance for all who sit at the table; there is solidarity with those who would otherwise have no table; there is companionship for the journey beyond the table.

Rehearse the Feast

In his book, *Bowling Alone*, Robert Putnam notes that, over the last three decades, there has been a 33 percent decrease in the number of families that share meals together. Of those families that still eat together, more than half of them do so while watching television. The typical American family eats together three times per week, with an average meal lasting no more than 20 minutes. Over that same period of time, there has been a 45 percent decline in the frequency of entertaining friends in one's home.

More often than not, we are eating alone, even in the presence of others.

We need to get out more, and we need to bring others in more. The vision of the Kingdom Feast in Revelation 7 has its origin in the prophecy of Isaiah 25, where all are welcomed, all are fed, and all are reconciled to God and to one another:

> On this mountain the Lord of hosts will make for all peoples a feast of rich food, a feast of well-matured wines,
> of rich food filled with marrow, of well-matured wines strained clear.
> And he will destroy on this mountain the shroud that is cast over all peoples,
> the sheet that is spread over all nations;
> he will swallow up death for ever.

Then the Lord God will wipe away the tears from all
faces,

and the disgrace of his people he will take away from all
the earth,

for the Lord has spoken.

It will be said on that day,

Lo, this is our God; we have waited for him, so that he
might save us.

This is the Lord for whom we have waited; let us be
glad and rejoice in his salvation (Isaiah 25:6-9).

The hospitable life is one that rehearses this future feast in
the here and now—with family, with friends, with strangers—
building bridges of understanding by which the grace of God
can move, heal, and restore us.

At the Kingdom table, a lavish feast is prepared for all
peoples.

At the Kingdom table, the shroud of hate and exclusion is
destroyed.

At the Kingdom table, the tears of violence are wiped away
from all faces.

At the Kingdom table, death and its acolytes are swallowed
up.

At the Kingdom table, every sign of disgrace is removed.

At the Kingdom table, there is gladness and joy in the
salvation of the Lord.

The hospitable life is one that sets this table daily in the
world.

Pull Up a Chair

An extraordinary model for this can be found in the creative initiative called Out to Dinner.[26] Out to Dinner is an annual outreach project that seeks to bring together gay and straight couples for the purpose of sharing a single meal, getting to know one another, and forming friendships. The organizer behind this initiative is Zach Wahls, a twenty-year old *straight* man and son of a committed lesbian couple from Iowa. After reflecting on his own life and realizing the effect his moms had on others when they were simply being themselves, Wahls discussed the notion with a number of national organizers, and the project was born. "There's a lot of misunderstanding about what it means to be a gay, lesbian, bisexual or transgender person or to have an LGBT parent or parents," said Wahls. "By bringing people together to just break bread and get to know each other, I think we can dispel some misconceptions." Out to Dinner does not ask participants to "have the talk" about sexual orientation or the political, social, theological issues related to being gay or straight; instead, it encourages guests to simply get to know each other in a spirit of gentleness and reverence toward the other.

Zach Wahls set the table.

Another creative model for rehearsing the Kingdom Feast is found in the local San Diego program called Fill-a-Belly.[27] In April 2008, Molly McKeown was walking in the Village of Carlsbad, CA, when she was approached by several homeless men asking for a meal or money to buy food. Having nothing to give them, Molly continued on her walk, but her eyes had been opened to the needs of the homeless in the community. She had never noticed them before: a group sitting at the fountain, a man sleeping at the Coaster rail station, a woman walking her bike down the sea wall. Distressed by the number of people who approached her, and heart-broken that she had nothing to give them, Molly began to consider what she could do. A simple idea finally presented itself: "I have a kitchen, I can cook." She offered the idea to her sister, Morgan, who saw it as an opportunity to get people involved in the community. The two sisters' outreach program began with handing out sack dinners in 2008. Today, it has grown into an operation spanning two cities, offering friendship and a warm meal to nearly 200 people a week. "Every person wants to be known by someone else," says Molly, "to know that they are cared about and not invisible or worthless." At Fill-a-Belly everyone eats together, volunteers and guests alike. They build relationships through sharing a meal, playing games and talking with each other.

In the end, both Out to Dinner and Fill-a-Belly are glimpses of the Kingdom Feast and acts of Communion. If they seem like more than you can handle right now, don't worry. You can start much smaller. You don't have to venture very far, as I have learned.

I met a friend for lunch not long ago. We sat outside in a large, crowded courtyard, surrounded by dancing fountains and barefoot children and Labradors on leashes tied to strollers. While the two of us were talking over lunch, I watched a disheveled man walk from table to table, asking guests for spare change. He wore a pair of old, worn-out combat boots, faded sweat pants with one hole in the right knee, a red flannel shirt that was slightly too small. He hadn't shaved in a million years or more. It was early August, under full sun.

I watched him as he moved from table to table, undeterred by rejection. He must have asked a dozen people, each of them shaking their heads politely before returning to their conversations. When he made his pitch to two women sitting a few tables to our left, one of them pulled out an empty chair and invited him to sit down. She shook his hand while the other woman handed him a menu. When the server arrived, he ordered a meal. "You can just add it to our check," I heard one of them say.

For the next thirty minutes, the three of them shared stories, broke bread in each other's company, and practiced the generous welcome of God.

Do This In Remembrance of Me

You need to get out more, pursuing the hospitable life in your own neighborhood by rehearsing the Kingdom Feast with your family and friends, and with strangers. Set the table as God has set the table for you. Live out the Eucharistic prayer spoken every time Christians gather around the Communion table: "May these gifts of bread and wine be for us the body and blood of Christ, that we may be for the world the body of Christ, redeemed by his blood."

In a competitive culture of ambition and achievement in which people are desperate to succeed in the Inner Ring, Communion is the gift that reminds us to rest in the finished work of Christ. In a fragmented culture that is radically individualistic and exclusivist, Communion is the gift that reminds us that we belong to one another, and that all are welcomed. In a restless, discontented culture of constant striving, Communion is the gift that demands a joyful, grateful heart. In an acquisitive culture driven by narcissism and self-promotion, Communion is the gift that calls forth a spirit of humility, generosity, and service.

You need to get out more. To practice Communion. To rehearse the Kingdom Feast. To set the table, expand your guest list, and break bread with those whom Jesus welcomed. As Tim Chester says, "Jesus didn't say, 'Think this in remembrance of me.' The Lord's Supper serves its purposes not when it's written about in books, but when it's shared in the Christian community."[28]

Hospitality Apps

Adventures in the Neighborhood

1. Create an imaginary guest list. Reach for a single sheet of paper and a pencil, and write up a guest list for an imaginary Kingdom Feast. At the top of the list, write the name, "Jesus." Now, identify twelve more guests that you will invite to this Kingdom Feast, according to the following criteria: (a) the first three guests on your list will be people you'd least like to share a meal with, such as enemies, those who have hurt you or those from whom you are estranged; (b) the next three guests will be people who are physically, spiritually, or emotionally hurting, such as your neighbor who's undergoing chemotherapy, the grieving widow at church, an alcoholic friend, a parent with Alzheimer's, the man on the corner holding the "Disabled Vet" sign; (c) the next three guests will all be children whom you especially love and who bring you particular joy, such as your own children, or grandchildren, or those of your friends or neighbors; (d) the last three guests will be people who do not share your particular religious convictions, such as an agnostic or atheist co-worker, a Jewish or Muslim friend, a Buddhist neighbor.

    Now that the list is complete, reflect on each person—their needs and joys, their hopes and dreams, their aches and awes. Imagine them sitting around the table of the Kingdom Feast in the presence of Jesus—invited, welcomed and accepted completely by the gracious host. Imagine the conversations that are taking place around the table, the sights and sounds and smells. Take note of how you're feeling as you observe what is happening around the table. Are you thankful, apprehensive, disappointed, hopeful? Offer these feelings to God in prayer.

Finally, consider the possibility of this imaginary feast becoming a reality in your home. What personal challenges preclude you from hosting such a feast? How might such a feast change your relationships with these guests? How might it change your relationship with God?

2. Attend a Jewish Passover Seder. Most local Jewish communities in the Reform tradition welcome non-Jews to their annual Passover Seder meal. While the Seder is not specifically a celebration of the Kingdom Feast, it is a memorial feast that celebrates the exodus of the Jews from Egypt, with rituals and foods symbolizing the dual themes of slavery and liberation. Attending a Seder as a guest is a powerful reminder of the generous welcome offered by others, the importance of community in the journey of faith, and the beauty of a well-told story passed down from generation to generation.

3. Host a neighborhood viewing of the film *Babette's Feast*, a wonderful story of an eighteenth-century Christian community in Denmark that has lost its way, becoming joyless and legalistic. Babette is a refugee from Paris who comes to live with two sisters. For twelve years she serves as their housekeeper, learning how to prepare their humble food. Then she wins ten thousand francs (each year a friend renews her Paris lottery ticket, and this year her number has come up). Babette asks if she can prepare a banquet for the community. She serves up course after course of the most exquisite food. One guest exclaims he has only ever tasted food like this at the famous Café Anglais in Paris. As the meal unfolds, the community rediscovers joy. Old feuds are ended. Confessions are made. The evening concludes with the community gathered around the village fountain singing the old songs of faith. Meanwhile the two sisters find Babette in the

chaos of the kitchen. She confesses, "I was once cook at the Café Anglais." "We will all remember this evening," the sisters say, "when you have gone back to Paris." But Babette has spent all the ten thousand francs on the feast and will not be returning to Paris.

4. Host a meal in your home, at the beach, or in a park. A few suggestions: (a) Keep it Simple. Hosting is about the experience, not the presentation. Prepare a meal that allows you time to visit, not one that takes you away from your company; (b) Be Authentic. Give your true self to your guests, free of the need to impress; leave the china in the cupboard and use your everyday dishes; (c) Request A Dish. It is completely appropriate to ask your guests to bring something, if they are able; (d) Communicate Expectations. When you are inviting people into your home, let them know you want to have them over so you can get to know them; if you have a specific agenda, let them know in advance; (e) Tell Stories. Be prepared to share about yourself, and to provide opportunities for your guests to tell their stories; (f) Show Pictures. Pictures are a great way to share your life with someone, stimulating and encouraging conversation; (g) Pray. Be prepared to offer a simple prayer before the meal, acknowledging God's goodness and generosity in providing food and friends at the table.

5. Spend part of your day baking bread. Share the loaves with your neighbors, your mail carrier, the UPS man, the street sweeper, etc.

6. Fast for twenty-four hours to remember the two billion people worldwide who live on less than a dollar a day.

"Be not simply good; be good for something."
—Henry David Thoreau

5

Abide

HOW WILL YOU CHOOSE to live your life today? To what end will you use the time, talents, and resources that you have been given? Will you get involved? Will you risk disappointment, set backs, even put yourself on the line, for the common good? Will you love this world with both body and soul, or will you turn inward and worry only about yourself?

The hospitable life adopts a rhythm of advance and retreat, of engagement and detachment, of cause and pause. Throughout the gospels, we see this guiding rhythm in the life and ministry of Jesus. After his baptism, but before he begins his earthly ministry, he is led by the Spirit into the wilderness to pray, to fast, to reflect on his life's purpose, to confront the powers and principalities of this world (Mark 1). After he feeds a crowd of 5,000 hungry followers, he retreats to the mountainside, alone, to be re-gathered by God (Matthew 14). On one occasion, after he predicts his ultimate fate on the cross to his disciples, Jesus takes his three best friends on a mountain retreat, to kindle the flame of faith and trust among them (Luke 9). On another occasion, nearly overwhelmed after having responded to so many chronic needs among the hungry, the poor, the ill, Jesus heads for the lake, boards a boat, and finds solitude, rest, and re-creation (John 6).

Wilderness, desert, lakeside, mountaintop. Jesus' life was shaped by intentional routines of retreat, detachment, and disengagement from the world. His life and ministry depended on getting away, momentarily, from the needs and demands and expectations of others. He understood that there are times to engage the world and make a difference, and times to disengage in order to reflect on what kind of difference one is making.

You need to get away more—alone and with others, for prayer, reflection, correction, re-orientation. To be a gracious host in the world, to practice healthy hospitality, you must learn to sit at the feet of Jesus, as a guest, to be fed by his word, sustained by his grace, emboldened by his power.

You need to get away more. But you can't stay away forever. For every retreat, there must be a corresponding advance. If you fail to re-engage the world, your disengagement will gradually fade into a defensive, dispassionate entrenchment that forsakes the call to take up the hospitable life.

The Creeping Normal

We're well practiced in the art of getting away and staying away, especially when we are hurting, or disillusioned, or fearful. Whenever we come up against something dark and terrifying that leaves us disillusioned about the world and our place in it, it's not uncommon for us—in fact, it is quite natural for us—to run with whatever strength we have left in search of whatever safe place still remains and take cover from the rest of the world. This is not spiritual retreat. This is defensive withdrawal. We pull the blinds and deadbolt the doors to keep the world out. We suddenly keep at a safe distance those whom we do not know. The familiar routines and simple pleasures that once gave our lives purpose no longer hold meaning. Those familiar places which once gave us a sense of belonging in the world no longer feel like home to us, and what we feel is something like a spiritual homelessness, a longing for the home we once had but we fear we may never get back.

Over the last decade, our sense of "home" has been irreversibly shaken by two national crises. The terrorist attacks of September 11, 2001 for many Americans shattered a treasured sense of what some have called American Exceptionalism—the notion that we Americans are a special people, qualitatively different from others in the world, buoyed by a unique destiny, guarded by providence, inherently good. On the Sunday following the attacks on the World Trade Center and the Pentagon, churches across the nation swelled with unprecedented crowds of people seeking comfort, solace, and answers to questions such as: How could this have happened? Where was God? Does God care? What are we, as a nation, to do in response? Is retaliation justified? How am I to now live my life?

The questions seemed so urgent at the time. Those asking them seemed so poised for change and re-orientation of their lives and priorities. But many of those who asked such questions gradually retreated, never to advance and re-engage. Curiously, the five largest mainline Protestant Christian denominations in the U.S. report steep declines in average worship attendance in the eight years following the attacks: United Methodists (10.22%), Episcopalians (17.86%), Lutherans (15.41%), Presbyterians (15.62%).[29] Today, worship attendance in mainline Christian churches is, on average, lower than it was prior to September 11, 2001. Perhaps the church, in the days after September 11, failed to speak a relevant, faithful word to those who were asking urgent questions. Perhaps the word that was spoken by the church fell on deaf ears, or offended the listeners.

Seven years after the attacks, by late 2008, the all-consuming pursuit of the American Dream succumbed to the fierce, unrelenting realities of the Great Recession as Americans, in record numbers, lost their homes, their jobs, and their savings at an unprecedented rate. The long season of unbridled prosperity came to an end, replaced by a period of scarcity (both perceived and real), uncertainty, and shattered dreams.

For many Americans, it has been a decade of unforeseen loss, desolation and disorientation, followed by a season of "homelessness" and, for some, hopelessness. The prevailing view suggests that this is the "new normal"—things are different; there is no going back to the way things used to be.

Welcome to Babylon

In the Bible, this sense of "homelessness" is called exile. Nearly one-third of the Bible is dedicated to describing that experience of exile in very honest and candid detail.

Anyone who has ever grieved deeply in the face of real loss knows something of what the Psalmist felt when, while in the midst of a long exile, he says in Psalm 137, "We sat down by the waters of Babylon and we wept when we looked back, when we remembered what our lives used to be like. We put away our harps because it seemed that our singing days were over. We said, 'How could we possibly sing the Lord's song in exile?'"

Anyone who has ever given themselves completely to some great cause, some high calling in life—a marriage, parenthood, a career, or an important cause—only to see it fail, or to experience disappointment, knows something of what it was like for Isaiah who, in exile, looks back at all of his hard work and says, "I have labored to no purpose; I have spent my strength in vain and for nothing" (Isaiah 49).

Anyone who has ever been victimized by evil or injustice, or suffered abuse at the hands of another, knows something of the righteous anger expressed by the Psalmist in exile, who says, "O Babylon, you are doomed to destruction, and happy is he who repays you for what you have done to us" (Psalm 137).

Exile is a universal human experience. Disappointment, disillusionment, detachment. Pull the blinds. Lock the doors. Accept the new normal. Be guarded about the future.

Make Yourselves at Home

In the 29th chapter of Jeremiah, the prophet has a surprising word for the people living in exile in Babylon. Judah has been defeated in battle, the holy city of Jerusalem has been leveled, the sacred Temple has been reduced to rubble. The religious leaders, the artisans, the merchants have mostly been killed, and those who survived have been driven across the desert by their captors, to live in settlements and refugee camps in Babylon. They are stripped of family, of faith, of land.

Their situation could not be more bleak and hopeless, and so they convince themselves that the only way to cope with their grief and homelessness is to withdraw emotionally and physically from their new reality—to seek solace in the memories of their past, in the old prayers and liturgies, to escape from the humility and degradation of their captivity by going inward, into the safe havens of the human spirit. It's a natural defense mechanism that is all too familiar to those who are religious. When the world seems unbearable, faith offers a comfort and even an escape, and many of the prophets who wrote to them in their exile were quick to write the prescription: "Hunker down," they said to the exiles. "Your captivity, your homelessness will not last long. You'll be home soon enough. Your liberation is coming. Just stay strong, cling to your faith, don't get too comfortable with Babylon. Don't let Babylon corrupt you. Protect yourselves."

The prophets were saying that since Babylon is not where you belong, don't make it your home. Sit back, hold out, withdraw. Do not engage outsiders. Protect yourselves. Wait it out.

But along comes Jeremiah, one of their less popular, relatively unknown prophets who, while remaining in the plundered rubble of Judah, writes the exiles a letter that contains an entirely different message. Jeremiah says, "Do not let the prophets and diviners among you deceive you. Do not listen to the dreams you encourage them to have. They are prophesying lies to you" (Jeremiah 29:8-9).

Instead of withdrawing further from their world and waiting it out, Jeremiah proposes an alternative plan. He tells them that they will be in Babylon for a very long time—too long, in fact, to withdraw from the world. He suggests that, while Babylon may not be their true home, it's where they will be planted for a while. So, he advises,

> Build houses and settle down; plant gardens and eat what they produce. Marry and have sons and daughters; find wives for your sons and give your daughters in marriage, so that they too may have sons and daughters. Increase in number there; do not decrease. Also, seek the peace and prosperity of the city to which I have carried you into exile. Pray to the Lord for it, because if it prospers, you too will prosper (Jeremiah 29:5-6).

Jeremiah's message was counter-intuitive. Get involved, pray for the city, add to the beauty, even in the sadness and desolation of your own exile. Make your neighborhood a home, because as the neighborhood goes, so goes your own happiness and peace.

Bloom Where You are Planted

There was a day when the Church had a central role—often a leading role —in social movements and the transformation of society for the common good. Whether advocating for the abolition of slavery, or for the right of women to vote, or for the civil liberties of people of color, the Church led the way, sometimes reluctantly, but generally with courage and resilience.

Today, Christians seem either increasingly silent in the face of so many escalating social problems—like poverty or hunger or equality—or they have grown increasingly obsessed with issues of personal morality. Like those exiles in Babylon, the Church has found the way of withdrawal and self-preservation to be safer than a genuine engagement with the real problems of our world. Too many Christians are saying, "Let's just keep this all about our spirituality, and let the world solve its own problems. Religion and politics don't mix. We come to church to get away from all that for a while."

But Jeremiah issues a call to action for us. What he says to us is unmistakably clear: *bloom where you are planted.* Do not withdraw from the world and retreat into your own ghetto, but love the world in which you find yourself. Serve your community in tangible, practical ways. Plant gardens. Build houses and live in them. Invest yourselves in genuine community. Make neighbors. Bloom where you are planted. Seek the welfare, the "shalom," the peace of the city because, in the end, your own peace and wellness is intricately and wonderfully woven into fabric of your neighborhood.

Seized by Passion

In July 1943, a frightened 17-year-old conscript in the German army took cover as Allied bombs rained down on his hometown of Hamburg, killing 40,000 people. He had been raised in a well-educated, non-religious, secular German home, but his experience in the bombing of Hamburg and his survival as a prisoner of war compelled him to ask the hard questions of life. While in captivity, he questioned the existence of God, the nature of God, the activity of God in the world. Does God know about this? Does God notice? Does God care? In time, mentored by a chaplain and nurtured by a fellowship of Christians in the camps, Jürgen Moltmann became convinced that God was so deeply committed to the life of the world that

God's own Son died on its behalf. He became a Christian. He later enrolled in theological school and became one of the most influential theologians of our time.

At the heart of Moltmann's theology is the principle of passion—God's passion for the world embodied in the life and death of Jesus Christ, and our passion, our command from God to love the world and be involved in the world in deeply incarnate ways. He writes,

> If we want to live today, we must consciously will life. We must learn to love life with such a passion that we no longer become accustomed to the powers of destruction. We must overcome our own apathy and be seized by the passion for life.[30]

Plant Gardens

A colleague of mine tells the story of a widow in her later years, living in Los Angeles during the time of the Uprising in 1993. She lived in a small house in the heart of where the most intense rioting and burning had taken place. To the left of her home was a building that had been nearly burned to the ground. To her right were several other small homes that had also been burned. Nearly the entire block had sustained damage from the fires.

During the first week of rioting she locked herself in her house, not knowing what to do, fearing for her life, grieving for the city. When the rioting and burning had finally subsided, she opened her door and walked outside. She wept as she beheld the devastation of her neighborhood. She didn't know what to do, but she began to reflect on who she was, what she cared most about, and what God would have her to do. Knowing that she had to do something, yet still too afraid to go outside her gated yard, she went back inside, grabbed several packets of vegetable seeds, and began to plant seeds in the bare soil and ash that was her front yard.

Soon, children from the neighborhood began to join her. They raked, they watered, and they planted more seeds in the soil. Before long, her entire front yard had been sown. For several weeks the children of the neighborhood would help her water and care for the garden, and when it came time to pick some of the ripened vegetables, she gathered the children around her, and she gave each of the vegetables names: "These," she said, "are 'Righteous Radishes,' and these green beans are 'Gracious Green Beans.' These are 'Tenacious Tomatoes,' and these are 'Peace-loving Peppers.'" She gave all of them names: "Charitable Artichokes," "Compassionate Carrots," "Zealous Zucchini," "Saintly Squash."

Bloom where you are planted. Build houses, plant gardens, make neighborhoods, engage the world. "Seek the welfare of the city, for in its welfare you will find your welfare."

Find Your Purpose

The retreat is over. It's time to advance, re-engage, bloom. Where do you begin? As Frederick Buechner has notably suggested, "The place where God calls you is the place where your deep gladness and the world's deep hunger meet."[31]

Look at the world around you, or your own little corner of the world, and identify a need. If your eyes are open, you will not have to look very far. But if you're not sure how to do that, if nothing comes immediately to mind, then ask yourself, "What is it about the world that I often complain about, or that keeps me up at night, or that breaks my heart?"

Take a moment to write down the needs that come to mind. Maybe it's the kids in your school district that go to school hungry, or the kids that come home from school to an empty house, or the kids that cannot read or write. Perhaps it's the seniors who live in lonely convalescent rooms; or the convicts who live in lonely prison cells; or the homeless, who are equally as lonely but have no place at all to live.

Look at your own little world, and find a deep need. Just pick one.

And then look at your life—your capable, gifted, passionate, blessed life—and ask yourself, "What do I have to give? What do I love to do? What is my passion? What is my unique gift which, when given to that special need in the world, gives me joy?"

Can you teach, or can you cook, or can you pick up trash at the beach, or listen to the lonely, or sit with the sick or the dying, or sweep floors, or wash feet, or pray on bended knee? What can you do?

Bruno Serato has a very successful Italian restaurant in Orange County near Disneyland. In 2005 Serato happened to take his mother with him to visit the local Boys and Girls club when we came upon a little boy eating potato chips for dinner. He learned that the boy, like most of the kids in the program, were motel kids. They attended this afterschool program at the club because the alternative was to be surrounded by the drugs and prostitution and violence of the motel culture.

Disturbed by the image of that boy eating potato chips for dinner, Serato committed himself to feeding these children. He said that it was the worst timing: when the recession started, his customer base plummeted, and the number of hungry motel children doubled. But he made this commitment to feed them—not leftovers from his restaurant, but fresh, specially prepared pasta for the children.

Seven days a week, he feeds 200 hungry motel children. He says, "I started doing this because my mama made me. But now I can't stop."[32]

What is your passion? What is your unique gift which, when given to that special need in the world, gives you joy?"

Take that gift of yours, apply it to that need in the world, and you have just discovered how it is and where it is that God is calling you today—you have just practiced the hospitable life.

Ignore Pedigrees

The pedigree of honey
Does not concern the bee;
A clover, any time, to him
Is aristocracy. [33]
-- Emily Dickinson

Are you wondering if you have what it takes, if you're qualified, credible? You're not alone. Consider the story of Rachel Lloyd, the author of, *Girls Like Us: Fighting for a World Where Girls Are Not For Sale*. In 1998, with no college degree, a borrowed computer, and $30, Rachel established Gems-Girls.org: Girls Educational and Mentoring Services, to support girls and young women victimized by the commercial sex industry. GEMS is now the nation's largest organization offering direct services to domestic victims of commercial sexual exploitation and trafficking. Rachel's trailblazing advocacy has led to groundbreaking legislation in New York, and is the subject of the critically-acclaimed Showtime documentary "Very Young Girls." She has helped more than 1500 girls and young women rehabilitate their lives over the last fourteen years.

Nobody ever authorized, credentialed, or licensed Rachel Lloyd to do the work she is doing. None of the 1500 women she has helped seemed to care about her resume. What mattered most to them, she says, was her own life story. Her personal experience of recovery and redemption became the only credential she has ever needed. For the vast majority of the women she works with, Rachel Lloyd was the first woman they'd ever met who actually made it off the streets.

Few people really care about your resume these days. What is most compelling to them is what you have done: your personal victories, your story, your body of work. This is why, when John the Baptist asked Jesus if he really was the Messiah, or if he should keep looking, Jesus replied: 'You tell me—the lame walk, the blind see, the dead are raised' (Luke 7:22).

You don't need a resume or a degree to live the hospitable life; nor do you need to be perfect. Jesus' disciples were ordinary people who heard an extraordinary call on their lives to follow and serve.

The way of hospitality is marked by humility and honest self-awareness. It is absent of ego and self-justification. Like the generous clover that hosts the sojourning honeybee, it knows its innate beauty and purpose. It stretches daily toward the sun, and yields to the guest.

This is your task—to stretch, to yield, and to leave the rest to God.

You have everything you need to feed the honeybee. Whatever you lack, God will provide you.

The Gospel According to Tim

"There is no passion to be found playing small," said Nelson Mandela, "in settling for a life that is less than the one you are capable of living." You must make a conscious choice to shun self-doubt and insecurity about your weaknesses and shortcomings, trusting that God's strength is made perfect in our weakness.

A few years ago *The Los Angeles Times* ran a compelling story about a homeless man in Compton who resurrected a Little League baseball program that had died more than thirty years ago. Tim Lewis grew up playing baseball at Compton's Sibrie

Field. While a few of his friends went on to play professional baseball, Lewis instead took the long, destructive road of addiction. In the process, he lost everything—his family, his job, his home. He now lives in his 1993 Toyota Camry, which he parks across the street from the baseball field. Lewis has been clean and sober for more than a year; he found a church community that has loved him back to life; he prays and reads his Bible daily.

On his journey back to life, he has found a passion and purpose: to restore the game of baseball to this small neighborhood that has been over-run by drugs and gang violence. In 2009, Lewis petitioned the Mayor of Compton, organized fundraising efforts, obtained a Little League charter, and recruited more than eighty players from the local elementary schools. He restored the ball field, once riddled with weeds and gopher holes, to playable condition. To many of the kids in the program, Lewis has become a father figure. He prays with them before every game, encourages them, teaches them life lessons, using his own troubled past as Exhibit A of what not to do. His sense of purpose and mission is unmistakable: "God delivered me and gave me something to do for these kids," he says.[34]

Stay a While

We live in a culture of the quick savior. Too many people come and go as they wish, out of convenience, making a few small repairs to the neighborhood. But rarely does it last.

You need to get out more. And you need to stay longer. Not forever, perhaps, but long enough to bring more lasting change to the neighborhood. "When you go to a place," says Jesus, "stay there until you leave" (Matthew 10). It's not a redundant commandment. It means, "Be present. Fully present. When you're there, don't allow your mind, your heart, to be elsewhere. Give yourself to the place, the people, for the time that you have."

In the late fourth century, a sixteen-year-old boy, born of Celtic aristocracy, was living somewhere in the British Isles when he was taken by Irish warriors on a slave boat bound for the east coast of Ireland. His name was Patricius, the son of a civil magistrate and tax collector. As a child he had often heard the tales of raiders who captured children and took them "to the ends of the world." He was now one of those children.

Upon mooring in Ireland, the young captive Patrick was sold to a cruel warrior chief, whose opponents' heads sat atop sharp poles around his palisade in Northern Ireland. He lived like an animal, enduring long bouts of hunger and thirst. He was isolated from other human beings for months at a time. Having left his homeland as a nominal Christian, he now turned to the Christian God of his fathers for comfort and guidance.

During his six years of captivity, Patrick learned the culture of the Irish. He learned to speak their language, befriended his barbarian captors, and earned a certain captive freedom that few slaves had ever achieved.

After having received a vision from God one evening to board a ship and return home, Patrick somehow negotiated his way onto a ship sailing to Gaul, present-day France, where he immediately studied for the priesthood and later served more than twenty years as a faithful parish priest in England.

But at the age of forty-six, Patrick received another vision from God. In a dream, an angel appeared to Patrick, carrying letters from his former captors in Ireland. The letters pleaded with Patrick to return to Ireland and teach the Irish people the way of Christ. After praying about the dream for several days, Patrick was shortly thereafter ordained a Bishop and appointed to Ireland as the first missionary bishop to the Irish Celtic barbarians. In the years that followed, Patrick established more than 700 churches in Ireland, ordained at least 1000 priests, and converted approximately one-third of the entire population of

Ireland to Christianity. It is believed that he single-handedly brought an end to the Irish slave trade, established peace among the warring tribes, and modeled the Christian ways of generosity, peace, and faithfulness to the Irish people. He did it without a sword.

Patrick brought to Ireland a simple strategy. It wasn't a strategy of Christian imperialism or coercive evangelism. It was strategy of gentleness, presence, and sacrifice. He bloomed where he was planted. His model was simple:

> Go to the people
> Live among them
> Learn from them
> Love them
> Begin with what they know
> Build on what they have.[35]

Wherever you are planted, the choice is yours to bloom or not, to retreat or to advance, to be seized by passion or paralyzed by self-preservation, to come and go, or to stay a while.

Choose the way of hospitality. Put down roots. Improve the neighborhood. Make it a home.

Hospitality Apps

Adventures in the Neighborhood

1. Invite the neighborhood kids to host a lemonade stand. Offer to pay for all the supplies (cups, lemonade, ice, etc.). Email, tweet, or text message all of your friends; post an update on Facebook, encouraging all of your friends to stop by for a cup of lemonade. Invite the kids to donate the proceeds to a local charity or important cause of their choosing.

2. Establish or join a local community garden co-op. Grow not only fruits and vegetables, but flowers.

3. Coordinate with your neighbors to plant a community tree in your neighborhood, or in the city or town in which you live.

4. Mow your neighbor's lawn.

5. Add your spare change to as many expired parking meters as you can.

6. Read Andrew Blackwell's, *Visit Sunny Chernobyl: And Other Adventures in the World's Most Polluted Places*, a thoughtful and sometimes irreverent guide to visiting and learning about some of the most polluted and abandoned places on earth. Think about the places in your own community that are polluted, abandoned, or in otherwise serious disrepair. Learn more about the history of those places and the factors that may have led to their decline. Partner with neighbors and/or other community leaders to restore these places and return them to their beauty and usefulness.

7. Practice "retreat" by keeping the Sabbath. For one day a week, try living without your phone, Internet, television, and your credit cards. Fast from technology, from work, from spending. Do something that contributes to your heart and soul.

8. Volunteer at your local Habitat for Humanity affiliate. Many of the homes that are built by Habitat for Humanity are located on properties that were once abandoned and neglected by the community. Habitat's mission is not only to transform lives by building affordable homes for families, but to strengthen communities by improving the neighborhoods in which they live. Find your local Habitat affiliate at www.habitat.org.

Afterword

IF YOU'VE COME THIS FAR in the book, you may be feeling overwhelmed by the call to action I have placed before you. Take a deep breath and allow me to make my confession: I need to get out more. I am no expert at living the hospitable life. I am not nearly as good at practicing hospitality as I am at writing about it. I could give you plenty of very good excuses for why this is the case: that I'm a borderline introvert; that as an ordained minister, I tend to do so much in the name of Jesus that I don't have much left to give at the end of the day; that I have a family to care for, and bills to pay, a growing stack of books to read, and two heaping laundry baskets of clothes that I never seem to have time to fold.

If I grade myself on a sliding scale, I'm hovering right around a B- with this stuff. Put me in a room with some of the hospitable people mentioned in this book, and I'm barely passing. I know this about myself. It's why I wrote this book.

But, perhaps like you, I still like to think of myself as a hospitable person. For the most part, I'm open-minded, not easily intimidated by new ideas or anxious about unfamiliar people or experiences. Generally speaking, I am respectful of people of other cultures, races, religions, social classes. I have close friends on both sides of the political aisle. I give money to the guy holding the clipboard in front of Target. Sometimes, I help stranded motorists on the highway, tip more generously than I should, mow my neighbor's lawn.

What I'm saying is that I really do have the best intentions. Sometimes I even act on them. But more often than not, I miss—or neglect—the hospitable moments that arise nearly every day of my life.

I read that there are 46 million people who own gym memberships in the United States, yet less than 20% of them actually go to the gym. They buy the shoes, the spandex shorts and sweat pants, the work out towel and water bottle. They carry their gym card around in their wallets; their duffle bag sits in the back seat of the car, and whenever they look in their rear view mirror and see it, they feel pretty good knowing that they belong to a gym. They proudly tell people, "That's my gym." And while they do not actually go to the gym, they still consider themselves one of those "gym people." Just that thought alone feels almost as good as actually going to the gym.

Sometimes, we confuse our best intentions with our actions, because just intending to do something can feel almost as good as actually doing it. Many of us tend to live "almost" lives, or maybe the truth is, many of us are almost living—stuck between the life we intend to live, and the one we are actually living—in an "almost" world that is miles away from the Kingdom that Jesus intended for us.

"Almost" isn't working. We need to close the gap between our good intentions and our tangible actions.

Jesus spoke of a man who had two sons, both of whom he asked to go out into the vineyard and work. One of the sons, having the best intentions, said, "I'm already on my way, Father, you can count on me," and yet he never left the couch. The other son said, "I'm not going to the vineyard today," but later had a change of heart and, perhaps even to his own surprise, went to the vineyard.

"Now, which of the two," asks Jesus, "did the will of his father" (Matthew 21:31)?

When it comes to living a hospitable life, it's not laziness or lack of desire or lack of opportunity that becomes our greatest force of resistance. That's not why our "yes" so often turns into a "no." Whenever our yes becomes a no, I've come to see that it's because we have forgotten that we are, in the end, merely guests in this world. Like the ancient Hebrews, we are all sojourners passing through, in desperate need of the hospitality and generosity of others; like the early gentile Christians, we are all aliens and strangers to one another, in desperate need of acceptance and a community we do not deserve; like Supreme, holding a trash bag of his past in each hand as he stands on the corner of Sixth and San Pedro, we are all restless hearts in this world, all desperately trying to find a way home.

We tend to think of ourselves first as hosts, as though we already belong, as though we have already found what we have been looking for. But God knows we are merely guests, and so a Host has been sent into our neighborhood. Jesus, moved by love, has crossed a border to find us. Jesus, having listened deeply to our peculiar life story, has chosen to weave it into the fabric of his redemptive plot. Jesus, having set a place for us at the table of his Kingdom Feast, has fed us generously. Jesus entered our neighborhood, choosing to abide with us until the whole neighborhood began to look more and more like the Kingdom of God.

We are mere guests. God's hospitality in Christ has welcomed us, redeemed us, and empowered us by the Holy Spirit to extend that welcome to the world. Hospitality is the daily practice of sharing God's welcome with the world.

Every day of our lives is a day of decision. Will I live the hospitable life? Will I cross a border, even tear down a wall, to expand my neighborhood and the people who dwell in it? Will I listen deeply to the people I encounter there, learning their stories, knowing them as only God knows them? Will I set the table for them, sharing my bread with friends and strangers, creating a context for lasting companionship? Will I advance into my world, bloom where I am planted, and stay a while, until the neighborhood resembles more and more the Kingdom of God?

What will you do today to live a more hospitable life?

We need to get out more.

It will transform our lives.

It will change our world.

It will lead us to that place called home, where we'll find all the other restless hearts of the world.

Let's go.

About the Author

Rev. Mark Feldmeir is a United Methodist Minister, currently in his seventh year as Senior Minister at San Dieguito United Methodist Church, a congregation of approximately 1000 members in North San Diego County, CA. He also serves on the Board of Directors for San Diego Habitat for Humanity.

Mark has been a member of the Adjunct Faculty at Claremont School of Theology since 2004, where he teaches preaching. He has previously authored two books —*Testimony to the Exiles: Sermons for GenXers and Other Postmoderns* (Chalice Press, 2003), and *Stirred Not Shaken: Themes for an Emerging Generation* (Chalice Press, 2005). Mark has lectured at various conferences throughout the country on topics ranging from preaching, generational theory, evangelism, pop culture, and Christian hospitality.

He lives in Carlsbad, CA, with his wife, Lori, and three children.

The Hospitality Project

This small book is but one step in the direction of encouraging others to practice hospitality in their daily lives. Where do we go from here?

If you are a community leader—religious or otherwise—I invite you to contact me about using *You Need To Get Out More* as a resource for discussion and study in your community. Because this book is ideally suited for small groups and classes, I have written a companion study guide, available as a complimentary download, at www.thehospitalityproject.com. At this website, you can also get details about buying books at a discount for your small groups and classes, and learn about other opportunities to practice and share the hospitable life in your own unique context.

If you are simply interested in staying in touch please consider subscribing to my mailing list by visiting www.markfeldmeir.com. I promise not to flood your mailbox with excessive email and you can unsubscribe at any time.

Finally, I hope you will share your experiences, inspirations and resources regarding your own adventures in hospitality. This is what keeps me, and others, striving to do better.

Endnotes

[1] Frederick Buechner, *Whistling in the Dark: An ABC Theologized* (New York: Harper and Row, 1988), pp. 15-16.

[2] Cited in Letty M. Russell, *Just Hospitality: God's Welcome in a World of Difference* (Louisville: Westminster John Knox Press, 2009), pp. 101-102.

[3] Faith Popcorn, *The Popcorn Report: Faith Popcorn on the Future of Your Company, Your World, Your Life* (New York: HarperBusiness, 1992).

[4] Henri Nouwen, *Reaching Out: The Three Movements of the Spiritual Life* (New York: Doubleday Publishing, 1986).

[5] Margot Starbuck, *Small Things with Great Love: Adventures in Loving Your Neighbor* (Downers Grove, Illinois: IVP, 2011), p. 29).

[6] Rick King, "An Act of Kindness Pays Richly" (*The Los Angeles Times: Los Angeles, CA, November 22, 1997, Record Edition), p. 7.

[7] Cited in, *With All God's People: The New Ecumenical Prayer Cycle* (Geneva: WCC Publications, 1989), p. 131.

[8] Julien Smith, *The Flinch* (The Domino Project, AmazonEncore, Kindle Edition, 2011), pp. 354-360.

[9] Robert Frost, "Mending Wall" (published online, July 1999, by Bartleby.com).

[10] See, http://undocumented.tv/2011/blog/jesus-el-buen-coyote.

[11] See, http://archives.umc.org/interior.asp?ptid=1&mid=1817.

[12] Donald McCullough, *The Trivialization of God: The Dangerous Illusion of a Manageable Deity* (Colorado Springs: NavPress, 1995), pp. 31-33.

[13] Michael Lindval, *A Geography of God: Exploring the Christian Journey* (Louisville: Westminster John Knox Press, 2007), p. 126.

[14] See, Mark 6:1-6; Matthew 13:54-58; Luke 4:16-30.

[15] See, Matthew 28:16-20.

[16] See, http://rescue.org.

[17] See, Donald Miller, *A Million Miles in a Thousand Years: How I Learned to Live a Better Story* (Nashville: Thomas Nelson, Inc., 2009), p. 48. Miller's work on understanding ourselves as characters living a real story has inspired the pages that follow. Miller's emerging work on this topic can be found at www.donaldmilleris.com. Other works consulted for this chapter include, Janet Burroway, *Writing Fiction: A Guide to Narrative Craft*, Fifth ed. (New York: Addison Wesley Longman, Inc., 2000), and Syd Field,

Screenplay: *The Foundations of Screenwriting*, Third ed. (New York: Dell Publishing, 1994).

[18] See, A.J. Jacobs, ed., *What It Feels Like* (New York: Three Rivers Press, 2003).

[19] Frederick Buechner, *Telling Secrets* (New York: HarperCollins, 1991), p. 30.

[20] Donald Miller, *A Million Miles in a Thousand Years: How I Learned to Live a Better Story* (Nashville: Thomas Nelson, Inc., 2009), p. 248.

[21] See, http://nationaldayoflistening.org.

[22] See, http://prisonerpal.com.

[23] Leonard Sweet, *The Jesus Prescription for a Healthy Life* (Nashville: Abingdon Press, 1996), p. 113.

[24] Find the entire text of *The Inner Ring* at http://www.lewissociety.org.

[25] See, Mike Graves & Richard F. Ward, eds., *Craddock Stories* (St. Louis: Chalice Press, 2001), pp. 83-84.

[26] See, http//outtodinner.org.

[27] See, http//fillabelly.org.

[28] Tim Chester, *A Meal with Jesus: Discovering Grace, Community, and Mission around the Table* (Wheaton: Good News Publishers/Crossway Books, Kindle Edition), p. 124.

[29] Lovett H. Weems, "No Shows," at *The Christian Century*, online version, September 22, 2010.

[30] Jurgen Moltmann, *The Passion for Life: A Messianic Lifestyle* (Minneapolis: Fortress Press, 1978), p. 22.

[31] Frederick Buechner, *Wishful Thinking: A Theological ABC* (New York: HarperCollins, 1973), p. 95.

[32] Learn more about Bruno Serato's inspiring story at http://www.cnn.com/SPECIALS/cnn.heroes.

[33] R. W. Franklin, ed., *The Poems of Emily Dickinson* (Cambridge: The Belknap Press of Harvard University Press, 1999), p. 1650.

[34] See, http://www.latimes.com/sports/la-sp-compton-baseball27-2009may27,0,3884007.story?page=1&track=rss.

[35] See, George Hunter, *The Celtic Way of Evangelism: How Christianity Can Reach the West...Again* (Nashville: Abingdon Press, 2000), p. 120.

15662266R00071

Made in the USA
San Bernardino, CA
02 October 2014